Y0-BCL-025

JUSTICE
THAT *Heals*

═══════════════════════

ARTHUR PAUL BOERS

═══════════════════════

A Biblical Vision for Victims and Offenders

Epilogue by Ron Claassen
Study guide by Eddy Hall

Faith and Life Press, Newton, Kansas

Justice That Heals critiques the North American criminal justice system from a Christian perspective and offers new and exciting alternatives for victims, offenders, and society.

Copyright © 1992 by Faith and Life Press, Newton, Kansas 67114-0347. This publication may not be reproduced, stored in a retrieval system, or transmitted in whole or in part, in any form by any means, electronic, mechanical, photocopying, recording, or otherwise without prior permission of Faith and Life Press.

Unless otherwise noted, all Scripture quotations are taken from the New Revised Standard Version, copyright © 1990, by the Division of Christian Education of the National Council of the Churches of Christ in the United States of America, and used by permission.

Printed in the United States of America
95 94 93 92 4 3 2 1
Library of Congress Number 92-71357
International Standard Book Number 0-87303-184-9

Editorial direction for Faith and Life Press by Susan E. Janzen; Eddy Hall, editor; copyediting by Edna Dyck; design by John Hiebert; printing by Mennonite Press.

In memory of Karen Plexman Chaif, I offer my thanks to Fred and Anne Plexman for the ways they hearten and inspire me with their integrity, love, bravery, and long-suffering in the most difficult of circumstances. I write this on behalf of my imprisoned friend, John Chaif.

Acknowledgements

The idea for this book grew from an informally organized group of people who work for several victim-offender action groups in Canada and the United States. The committee includes Dean Peachey, Harold Regier, Melita Rempel, Dave Worth, and Howard Zehr. A Schowalter Foundation grant enabled this committee to do several projects, including this book. Wholehearted thanks are due to the committee for the innovative, energetic, creative ways they have approached restorative justice. Thanks, too, to the Office of Criminal Justice of the Mennonite Central Committee U.S. for their support of this project.

Special thanks to Wayne Northey for helping develop an early outline for this book, contributing case studies, and making numerous suggestions about projects and questions for discussion. I also gratefully acknowledge the help and contributions of Ron Claassen, Marietta Jaeger, and Mary Stewart for sharing stories, ideas, and valuable resources. Besides the committee members mentioned, LeRoy Friesen, Skip Graham of St. Leonard's House, Dave Gustafson, and Alan Kreider also read an early draft of this book. Thanks as well to my editors on this project Maynard Shelly, Susan E. Janzen, and Eddy Hall.

The shortcomings here are all my responsibility. I feel privileged to have worked with all of the persons named here.

—Arthur P. Boers

Table of Contents

Introduction

O ne cold February night, a friend called me. His twenty-five-year-old sister had been murdered by people she never knew. He described the pain of the loss and the horrors of identifying her body. Later, he endured the despairing travail of going to court over and over, only to be frustrated each time.

Another evening a friend called me to tell me that a mutual friend had been killed with a rifle. Her husband, also my friend, was charged with the deed.

Another friend's whole life changed on the night that he was threatened with a gun.

I have sat with friends who have been raped or burglarized and have not known what to say. I have visited people in jails and prisons. I have mediated between victims and offenders. Some of my friends are victims of heinous crimes. Other friends are offenders or ex-convicts.

I have lived in neighborhoods where my neighbors were drug pushers, prostitutes, and members of street gangs. Other neighbors suffered as crime victims. I read in the newspaper of the crimes that happen within blocks of my home. And I am afraid.

All of us are affected by criminal justice issues. We may not know a murderer or a murder victim, but most of us know someone who has been robbed, burglarized, or raped.

All of us have watched the evening news or read a newspaper and been horrified by the crimes reported. We weep for the victims and are perplexed by the offenders.

We are all left confused when we encounter crime. It always seems senseless and purposeless. It unsettles and frightens us. We long for security and hope for answers.

But security and answers come neither quickly nor easily.

All the victims and offenders I know agree on one thing: they are all frustrated by their experiences. I have never met anyone—victim or offender, police officer or lawyer, probation officer or criminal justice activist—who is satisfied with the "system." No one feels adequately dealt with or properly treated. No one believes that the criminal justice system in Canada or the United States deals with the real issues. Everyone feels violated by the process.

For those in the middle class, the solution is obvious: go by the rules and try to avoid prosecution. Sometimes that works, but not always. One friend lived an uprightly middle-class life, but was still falsely accused and wrongly convicted of first-degree murder. Some go to great lengths to protect themselves from crime, investing in crime protection devices. Those who are nevertheless victimized inevitably feel assaulted, first by crime itself and then by an insensitive bureaucracy.

Trying to avoid the criminal justice system is not enough. Every day victims and offenders are drawn into its spheres of influence. And for them, two questions, as old as the Scriptures themselves, continue to haunt us: Who is my neighbor? The victim of crime? The perpetrator of crime? The other pertinent question is the one uttered by the first recorded murderer, Am I my brother's keeper?

We are not alone in struggling with these questions and confronting these fears. In this book, you will meet some of my friends and acquaintances, victims and offenders both. You will read tragic stories of destruction and dashed dreams, but also stories of hope and reconciliation.

We will hear what the Bible has to say to these issues—its words of hope, challenge, and counsel.

We will meet victims of crime and better understand the

needs and fears they contend with. We will be trained in compassion.

We will meet offenders, some unrepentant and others working hard to make things right, as well as those wrongly accused of offense. We will learn to see beyond our stereotypes.

We will be inspired by Christians throughout North America who are trying to implement a different form of justice. Their hope, their objective is restorative justice—a justice that brings healing to victims, offenders, and society. Their ideals have been fleshed out in concrete, workable programs that offer new and exciting alternatives. Many of their projects involve the eager participation of both victims and offenders.

CHAPTER 1

Who Is My Neighbor?

The Anguish of Victims

Just Another Burglary

Fifteen years ago in Toronto, Melanie had a horrifying experience. This is the story she told me.

As I turned the key in my apartment door, I heard something inside, but thought nothing of it and buzzed right on in. Just then a swivel chair overturned. A man walked in from the kitchen wearing one of my scarves around his face, from the top of his nose down, and tied at back. He closed the door and hooked the chain-lock.

I screamed.

"Sit down and shut up," he yelled.

I sat on the couch and glanced around the room. The TV had been pulled into the middle of the floor; wires had been torn off the stereo. A closet door stood open. Boxes were everywhere.

"Where are you going?" he demanded. I was just ready to leave for a vacation in Chicago, but I didn't say anything. "Who do you live with?" Still, I said nothing. "Are you expecting anybody?" My friend Diane was waiting for me downstairs. I'd just loaded my bags into her car. If she buzzed, would that help me break free, I wondered, or would it put her in danger too? But I didn't tell him about Diane.

He flipped open a switchblade. Its blade flashed as his unsteady hand brought it to my face once, twice, but he didn't touch me.

I was furious. This was my holiday, and this guy was robbing me of it! If I could just get hold of one of those bricks from my bookcase, I schemed, I could do this guy in.

"Start packing these things in these boxes," he ordered. I played along in hopes of getting hold of a brick. I bent down and got to work. He looked at me, then turned and went into one of the bedrooms.

It wasn't premeditated, but when I saw his back to me I got up, unlatched the door, and darted through. He came yelling after me. I don't know how long he followed me down the stairs. My scarf was found later in the stairwell.

I burst outside, screamed as loudly as I could, and fell against Diane's apartment two blocks away. One nightmare was over, but a different kind of nightmare was about to begin.

When I called the police, they were upset we had left the scene. When we got back to my high rise, the police made us go with them as they went up to check out the apartment. Three officers went up the stairs and two took the elevator with Diane and me huddling behind them.

There was not a soul in the apartment, but it was a mess. I was upset and didn't like being there. It didn't seem my place anymore. The police took fingerprints and asked a lot of questions. "What did he look like?" He had this mask, but I knew what his eyes were like and his build. "What color was his switchblade?" "What kind of spring did it have?" I wasn't up on switchblades. I just knew it had been pretty close to my face. "Did he physically harm you in any way?" He hadn't.

One older officer sat down beside me. "He wasn't going to harm you," he said. "He just wanted valuables and money. There's really nothing here that's worth anything anyway." I knew he was trying to be nice, but I was insulted. He went to put his arm around me to console me. I was really mad. I didn't want anybody touching me. I felt like my whole life had been invaded.

I had to go to a police station and check mug shots; then I went back to Diane's apartment. I was a wreck. We decided to stay the night at her place. I had to phone family members and try to be big and brave and not to be upset. That evening it was hard to sleep.

The next day we went to Chicago. When we ate at a dark

restaurant there, I felt afraid. I was sure people were following me and looking at me. Even when we went to a shopping mall in broad daylight, I was still upset.

When I returned to work at a hospital in Toronto, I had trouble making rounds at night. Whenever I needed to walk to the end of the hall where it was dark, I had to go with someone else. Then when I got home from work, I'd check behind all the curtains, even the shower curtain, leaving the front door open until I'd looked everywhere.

When I couldn't sleep, I got sleeping pills from the doctor. They zonked me, but then I had nightmares that people were in and out without my knowing about it. Everywhere I went, I carried an umbrella with a long sharp end on it. The building superintendent would ask me why I carried the umbrella. "You never know when it's going to rain," I'd say. He'd say, "Sure, sure."

About ten weeks later, I came home from work. It was almost midnight. I got on the elevator with my umbrella. There in the elevator stood the guy who had been in my apartment. He looked at me funny.

I got off on my floor and he followed me. I walked to my door, my keys in one hand and my umbrella in the other. I walked into my apartment and he walked into his—the apartment right across the hall from me.

I called the police. "You could never identify the person in court because of the scarf," they said.

But I knew it was him. "You'd be asking for trouble if you pursued this," he answered.

In three months, seven apartments were robbed in that building. An elderly lady was knocked out and her valuables taken. As it turned out, the guy had a master key and could get into all the apartments. I have no idea whether charges were filed, but the building superintendent was fired.

I considered moving, but knew I could be afraid wherever I was. So I stayed, but I never forgot about it.

Consequences of Victimization

Melanie's story is not unusual. Victims of crime often feel victimized several times over. Some who advocate tougher "law-and-order" think they are working for the interests of victims. In reality, victims are already abused and neglected by law-and-order. They need not more law and order, but a different kind of justice.

The first victimization is the crime itself. Most victims feel terrified and helplessly confused. Eventually other feelings emerge: rage, insecurity, guilt, suspicion, depression, and regret. A common result is sleeplessness, which contributes to exhaustion, which in turn lessens the ability to cope with intense emotions. Sometimes jobs are lost. One mother of a murder victim had a nervous breakdown and was still on medication four years later.

Rape survivors often have fears of the attacker's returning, being alone, being attacked again, contracting venereal disease, becoming pregnant, friends and relatives finding out, reporting the rape to police or hospitals, the consequences of reporting, returning to work or school, resuming relationships with men, and walking down the street.

Howard Zehr, director of the Mennonite Central Committee U.S. Office on Criminal Justice, describes common effects on victims.

Lack of sleep, reduced appetite, nervousness and a greater susceptibility to illness or accidents are common experiences following a crime. Victims sometimes begin to rely on alcohol and/or drugs in order to cope.

Financial losses may be important. The crime may result in losses of property or significant medical costs. Work time may be lost, resulting in reduced income.

Job performance often deteriorates. Victims and their loved ones may have difficulty concentrating on the job and may become erratic in their work habits. Depression, reduced efficiency and emotional outbursts may cause tension at work and result in reprimands from work supervisors.

Children may do poorly in school. They may become depressed, distracted or begin to "act out." They may withdraw emotionally and become uncommunicative. They may feel left out or unloved.

Marriages often become strained. One spouse may grieve differently and/or less obviously than the other, leading to tension and misunderstanding. Tension and even divorce is common following a serious crime.

Sexual interest and behavior are often affected. Interest in the sexual part of a relationship may be reduced or altered. Some may begin to "act out" sexually.

Special occasions may become difficult when they bring back memories, for example of a murdered loved one. Anniversaries of the crime may be painful. [1]

Zehr was for many years involved only with the offender side of criminal justice issues. It was through the Victim Offender Reconciliation Program [2] that his vision of God's justice came to grapple with the needs of victims as well.

Doug Magee has explored both sides of such issues. *Slow Coming Dark* (Pilgrim, 1980) is a series of painful interviews with prisoners on death row. A more recent book, *What Murder Leaves Behind: The Victim's Family* (Dodd, Mead, 1983), explores the problems of survivors. Through studying crime first from the perspectives of offenders and their families, Magee came to see how our society neglects victims.

How the System Fails the Victim

After the trauma of a crime, many victims are further shocked by the way they are treated or ignored. Police are often callous, cruel, or rude when dealing with victims. Zehr notes that "victims feel twice victimized, first by the offender, then by a process which has no time for victims." [3] Victims are often further harmed by insensitive intrusions of the press.

Police investigations can deepen the psychological wounds inflicted by the crime. This is notoriously so in cases of rape and other forms of abuse. One rape victim reported:

About a year ago I had the misfortune to find out just what police treatment is like in cases of rape. I was raped by a total stranger who hid himself in my car I. First [the police] took me to Swedish Hospital to determine if I had been raped (which I was billed for later). Then they took me to the police building for questioning. They asked me to write out a statement about what happened and then the first question they asked, "Was he Mexican?" Then, "Did you have an orgasm? Are you using birth control? Why are you using birth control? When did you start using it? Were you going with a guy at the time?" It seems to me that most of this is irrelevant to the fact of rape. [4]

Two coeds were terrorized by a prowler in the middle of the night. [5] The man stole watches, jewelry, and a wallet and left. The coeds dutifully called the police who were not at all pleased. They complained about the lack of physical evidence. The police were especially irritated that neither of them could describe the burglar except to say he was considerably under six feet tall and had carried a flashlight and a gun.

The next day a detective explained that there was not enough evidence to proceed with an investigation and implied that the coeds had exaggerated their story. It was not important enough a crime, even though there had been a series of similar burglaries. While the victims were trying to get over their shock, the police made them feel worse. The school then demanded that the girls keep quiet about the crime, fearing for the school's reputation.

It is bad enough when a crime's perpetrator remains anonymously "at large." Even when the offender is known, some serious crimes are not prosecuted because of a lack of judicially useful evidence or for other reasons. [6] William Ryan contends that "fewer than one in five of the major crimes (and an even smaller proportion of all crimes) ever lead to an arrest; and a large number of those arrested are never brought to trial."[7]

A friend of mine was raped. Several weeks later she saw her rapist on a city bus. Before she could decide what to do, he recognized her and got off the bus. Later, she saw him again, this time at the train station with a woman who appeared to be his newlywed bride. My friend did nothing, but each time she saw the man she felt the trauma of the rape again.

A woman was victimized by a burglar. The police made a report, indicating there was little to do. They didn't even take fingerprints.

Later that evening a detective came by. He said the police were sure they knew who had done it. The method of operation exactly fit a man who was out on bail after confessing to sixty-seven similar burglaries in the immediate neighborhood within the last year. It seems he had been caught red-handed in one of them and had made a deal with the police to clear their books. He described each burglary precisely.

In nine more days his prison term would begin. In the meantime he was out on bail. [8]

Unless the victim saw the offender with the stolen property, there was not enough evidence to prosecute him.

Victims are often shut out of the process and not informed of developments. "Bert Dixon's life changed forever the moment he saw his son's body on the television news. That's how he found out Kelly, 18, had been stabbed repeatedly in the back seat of his own car and dumped in a Halifax (Nova Scotia) parking lot." [9]

A decade ago I was a student volunteer with VORP (an extra-legal, volunteer organization) in Elkhart, Indiana. When I contacted victims and told them the offenders had been prosecuted, it was the first the victims even knew that the offenders had been caught.

John was attacked while washing his car; his arm was broken and his car stolen. The car was recovered, although damaged, and the offender arrested.

John and his wife were told that they would be kept informed on the progress of the case, but they were not. They missed virtually every important hearing either because no one told them the times and dates, or because the hearings were rescheduled without warning. The couple finally decided to meet the prosecutor to find out why they were being so badly treated. The answer they received was blunt: "You are not part of this case; you just happened to be the victims. This was an offense against the state, and that's how we handle it."

The official's brutally frank (and legally correct) answer shows how skewed the Western view of crime and justice has become. Rather than formally acknowledging that crime causes injuries to victims, our laws define it as only an offense against government. Victims are not parties in criminal cases. They are merely evidence for the prosecution. [10]

Victims are at the mercy and disposal of others. They can suddenly be asked by the police or the court to help identify stolen property or to appear in court.

Bert Dixon, the man who learned of his son's murder through the TV news, is bitter about his months-long court experience in which three people were tried and convicted.

"I didn't have anybody. . . . There were three Salvation

Army people with the accused ones. As far as me, it was: 'To hell with you. You don't have a problem. You're not going to jail or anything like that.'

"I was saying to myself: 'Oh God, this doesn't work.' It's just unbelievable how callous this system is." [11]

The victim's involvement in the criminal justice procedure is painful. Victims are often accused of bringing the crime on themselves. This is reinforced by the fact that a "common reaction of victims is . . . 'frozen-fear compliance.' Confronted by such a terrifying, overpowering situation, victims of violent crime frequently seem to cooperate with their oppressor. In some crimes such as rape, this natural psychological reaction may be misinterpreted by courts as willing collaboration. In actuality, however, such compliance is rooted in terror." [12]

Horror stories abound. In Canada, "a 74-year-old woman was forced to perform oral sex on a cab driver who had helped her carry groceries into her apartment. In court . . . the infirm woman was grilled because she didn't bite her attacker or knee him in the groin to prevent the assault while his hands were around her throat." [13]

Friends and family also sometimes blame the victim. Victims are often made to feel as if they somehow were partially the cause of the crime, but most victims have done nothing to deserve the crime.

Even when victims are included in the legal process, their involvement can be harmful. In court, a victim's credibility as a witness is often challenged: "Is it sure that this offense happened? Is it certain that your property was that valuable? Why did you go into the bar alone when you had that tight clothing on? Shouldn't you expect to be raped as a result?" [14]

Victims make a disturbing discovery. "Few communities have programs and people assigned to help victims. Police and courts have little time for victims. As a result, victims are usually forgotten." [15]

Crime is a huge problem. "Over 25 million households in the United States and Canada were reported to have been victimized by a crime of violence or theft in one recent year. Approximately 200,000 families were left to grieve the murder of a loved one during the past decade." [16] (When citing such statistics, the media often ignores the fact that most serious crimes are committed by acquaintances, not strangers.)

Lately, more attention has been paid to the needs and rights of crime victims. Anyone who has been moved by the parable of the Good Samaritan understands the Christian mandate to minister to victims. Numerous victims groups (e.g., Parents of Murdered Children, based in Cincinnati) have been formed throughout North America. Even so, much of the initiative for these developments comes from victims themselves. Society on the whole still resists giving priority to victims' needs.

Unfortunately, some victims-cause groups further polarize issues of criminal justice, focusing narrowly on only one concern: either reform alternatives for convicts or achieving rights and prerogatives of victims. While both are important concerns, we need to maintain a view of the "bigger picture," where both victims and offenders merit attention. Happily, many projects (such as Victim Offender Reconciliation Program, Justice Fellowship) recognize the need to work with both victims and offenders.

This dual emphasis is clearly biblical. In the Bible's first recorded crime, God empathizes deeply with the slain victim Abel. "Listen; your brother's blood is crying out to me from the ground" (Genesis 4:10b). At the same time God protects Cain the offender from capital punishment (Genesis 4:15). God's concern is for both victims and offenders and we must be similarly involved.

For Discussion

1. Do you think Melanie's experience was typical or unusual? Do you believe she was well treated? What needs did she have? How were her needs dealt with?

2. Have you—or anyone close to you—ever been the victim of a crime? What were your feelings? What needs were unmet? How was the situation resolved?

3. What are some of the consequences of victimization? Did any of the needs of victims surprise you? Which ones? In what ways do you think society could better meet the needs of victims?

4. Why are so many inclined to work only on behalf of victims or only on behalf of offenders? What motivations do we have as Christians to work for both?

5. What are some ways that the criminal justice system aggravates the wounds of victims?

6. Why are rape victims so hesitant to report victimization? How does the criminal justice system encourage such silence? Does this reflect a systemic bias against women?

7. Were you surprised at the obstacles to prosecution? Would you be bothered if the police were sure about who robbed you and yet did nothing? If so, why would this bother you?

8. Can victims be helped just by placing greater emphasis on forgiveness? Why or why not?

9. Why do victims need to be a part of the process? What are the hazards of such inclusion?

10. How can churches begin to meet the needs of victims?

11. Do you agree that victims need a sense of vindication? Why or why not?

12. How has society's definition of crime (as an offense against the state) contributed to the systematic exclusion of victims?

Aids to Reflection

I have never seen a victim satisfied by a court. Tonight I just heard from two.

—Judge Caeton, a Superior Court Judge for ten years, at the annual gathering of VORP of Central Valley California (*Criminal Justice Network Newsletter*, October 1989-March 1990).

To demonstrate why most rape victims prefer not to press charges, let's imagine a robbery victim undergoing the same sort of cross-examination that a rape victim does:

"Mr. Smith, you were held up at gunpoint on the corner of First and Main?"

"Yes."

"Did you struggle with the robber?"

"No."

"Why not?"

"He was armed."

"Then you made a conscious decision to comply with his demands rather than resist?"

"Yes."

"Did you scream? Cry out?"

"No. I was afraid."

"I see. Have you ever given money away?"

"Yes, of course."

"And you did so willingly?"

"What are you getting at?"

"Well, let's put it like this, Mr. Smith. You've given money away in the past. In fact you have quite a reputation for philanthropy. How can we be sure you weren't contriving to have your money taken by force?"

"Listen, if I wanted—"

"Never mind. What time did this holdup take place?"

"About 11 p.m."

"You were out on the street at 11 p.m.? Doing what?"

"Just walking."

"Just walking? You know that it is dangerous being out on the street that late at night. Weren't you aware that you could have been held up?"

"I hadn't thought about it."

"What were you wearing?"

"Let's see—a suit. Yes a suit."

"An expensive suit?"

"Well yes. I'm a successful lawyer, you know."

"In other words, Mr. Smith, you were walking around the streets late at night in a suit that practically advertised the fact that you might be a good target for some easy money, isn't that so? I mean, if we didn't know better, Mr. Smith, we might even think that you were asking for this to happen, mightn't we?"

—*American Bar Association Journal* as quoted in The Prison Research Education Project's *Instead of Prisons.*

A defense attorney stated: "As defense counsel we are not burdened with a lot of the obligations that prosecutors have. We have free reign to do practically anything we want, as long as it's legal. We will impugn the integrity of witnesses when

we really don't have any justification for impugning their integrity. . . . We can accuse victims of being promiscuous and highly immoral ladies, when in fact there is no justification for doing that. It's unfair, but our system builds unfairness. As a defense attorney, it's my job to exploit every opportunity for the defense of my client (the rapist). I'm not involved with the moral issues involved. . . . It's the image of our client and the image of the woman that goes into the mind of the jury that's important. It's not what the actual facts are."
—Quoted in The Prison Research Education Project's *Instead of Prisons.*

END NOTES

1 Howard Zehr, *Who Is My Neighbor?* (Mennonite Central Committee U.S. Office of Criminal Justice pamphlet), pp. 5-6.

2 "Victim-offender reconciliation or mediation is a process in which victim and offender are brought together by a trained mediator to discuss what happened in a criminal offense and to explore options for resolving the issues surrounding the offense. It is an alternative process available to judges, probation officers and prosecutors in dealing with criminal offenders, and can offer a total or partial substitute for jail or prison incarceration.

"Cases are usually referred to the Victim Offender Reconciliation Program (VORP) by the court and probation department, although referrals may be accepted from other criminal justice and community agencies.. After a referral is received and screened at VORP it is assigned to a trained community volunteer. The volunteer separately contacts the victim and offender, explaining the program, discussing the offense and its aftermath, and soliciting participation.

"If the offender and victim agree to meet each other, the volunteer sets and facilitates a meeting at which the facts of the case are discussed, the injustice (violation) is recognized, equity is restored through a negotiated agreement and future intentions are explored.

"After the VORP meeting, the contract and a written summary are sent to the referring agency for approval and enforcement. VORP staff monitor the case until fulfillment of the contract is verified. Although not practiced in all programs, one option is to then provide an opportunity for a final meeting which would take place when the contract has been completed in order to bring closure for all parties.

"Many VORPs deal mainly, but not exclusively, with property offenses, although some are designed for certain types of offenses against persons. As a sentencing alternative, VORP is not intended to be used as an additional penalty tacked on to a standard sentence. Participation in the program is intended to be voluntary; while VORP may be ordered as part of a criminal sentence or as probation condition, the referral will not be pursued if either victim or offender is unwilling. In the event that no agreement is reached at the meeting, options are explained and the case is returned to the referring agency" (*VORP Volunteer Handbook*, Mennonite Central Committee U.S. Office of Criminal Justice, p. 4).

3 Zehr, *Who Is My Neighbor?*, p. 3.

4 Quoted in Fay Honey Knopp et al, *Instead of Prisons* (Syracuse, N.Y.: Prison Research Education Action Project, 1976), p. 143.

5 This story and its uncited quotes are from Kit Kuperstock, *Worried About Crime?* (Scottdale: Herald Press, 1985), pp. 55-57.

6 See Kuperstock, *Worried About Crime?*, pp. 57 ff. for examples.

7 William Ryan, *Blaming the Victim*, Revised Edition (New York: Vintage Books, 1976), p. 201.

8 Howard Zehr, *The Christian as Victim* (Mennonite Central Committee U.S. Office of Criminal Justice pamphlet), p. 4.

9 "Victim channels anguish into anti-crime crusade," CP story, *Windsor Star* (Monday June 18, 1990), p. B6.

10 Daniel W. Van Ness, "Pursuing a Restorative Vision of Justice," in *Justice: The Restorative Vision* (Mennonite Central Committee Occasional Papers, No. 17, Feb. 1989), pp. 17-18.

11 "Victim channels anguish into anti-crime crusade," p. B6.

12 Howard Zehr, *Changing Lenses* (Scottdale: Herald Press, 1990), p. 20.

13 "Victim channels anguish into anti-crime crusade," p. B6.

14 Nils Christie, *Crime, Pain, and Death, New Perspectives on Crime and Justice* (Mennonite Central Committee U.S. Office of Criminal Justice, Occasional Papers No. 1, 1984), p. 9.

15 Zehr, *Who Is My Neighbor?*, p. 2.

16 Zehr, *Who Is My Neighbor?*, p. 2.

CHAPTER 2

Restoration or Retribution?
The Anguish of Offenders

The Criminal Who Didn't Belong in Prison

In the mid-seventies, twelve burglaries were committed in northern Indiana and southern Michigan. [1] Randy and Tanya Brown lost all their wedding gifts and had their home ransacked. Another family, Randy and Elizabeth Yohn, lost a TV, radios, tape recorders, a gun, and meat.

The Yohns experienced the normal anxieties and trauma of victims: "Who could have done such a thing? Why did they pick our house out of the entire neighborhood? Were they stalking us, or was our house selected randomly? Will they come back? What would have happened if we had come home while the crime was being committed? Did the criminal have a gun?"

Randy Brown had a more visceral wish: "At first, I wished that I had been home so that I could have shot him," he commented during the filming of an ABC television documentary. "It's just as simple as that."

Eventually the burglar was caught. Fred Palmer had dropped out of high school at seventeen. He fought in the Vietnam War, received several commendations including a Bronze Star, and was honorably discharged in 1970. During the war Palmer learned to kill and to steal (the latter when his unit needed certain equipment). In 1976 Palmer married but was never able to pay his bills. Palmer said that he turned to burglary because he "wanted his wife and daughter to have things like other people do."

In 1978 Judge William Bontrager sentenced Palmer to the mandatory sentence of ten-to-twenty years for first-degree burglary. Bontrager credited Palmer for the 159 days he had already served. Over the objections of the prosecutor's office, Bontrager conditionally suspended the rest of the prison sentence if Palmer would serve 205 days in maximum security prison, make restitution to his victims, undergo psychotherapy, and serve five years of probation.

This was a surprisingly light sentence from a judge who was known to be tough on convicted criminals. "Bontrager believed that a person like Fred Palmer who spends more than a year in prison is often destroyed. His intention, as told to *Newsweek,* was to give Palmer, 'a solid dose of maximum security and then bring him back while there was still time to work with him.' "

During his stay in a maximum security prison, Palmer became a Christian. After being released from prison, he worked at a low-paying job and endured several layoffs. The probation office referred him to VORP so Palmer could work out restitution with his victims. The Yohns were skeptical about Palmer but did meet him. The intense meeting resulted in a restitution agreement.

The Yohns were impressed by Palmer and became more impressed with him as they got acquainted when he came to make his payments. When Palmer had no money for Christmas gifts for his wife and daughter, Randy Yohn arranged for gifts to be given. "The Yohns' initial bitterness and anger from being victimized slowly developed into a sense of understanding and reconciliation with the very person who had violated them. Randy would even kid with Palmer about how perhaps he should watch their home while the Yohns were on vacation."

The Browns—especially offended by the loss of their wedding gifts—were more bitter. Randy Brown proposed bringing a shotgun to any meeting. But they too eventually met with Palmer. Once again, restitution was arranged. Palmer met other victims as well. "When I faced my victims, it scared the living daylights out of me and it hurt. I done wrong. I would at least like to pay them back some way." Palmer's probation officer noted that "Fred has made extremely good efforts toward becoming a productive member of his community."

In spite of Palmer's progress at home, on the job, and with his victims, and in spite of the satisfaction of his victims, a larger tragedy was in process. The prosecutor's office remained unhappy with the sentence and contested it in the Indiana Supreme Court. In March of 1979, that court ruled that the local court could not suspend the prison sentence. Bontrager disqualified himself from the case and considered resigning. As one trained in Christian faith, he noted the "irreconcilable differences between the laws of Indiana and the laws of God." He was persuaded to remain as a judge. In September, Palmer was sentenced to ten-to-twenty years in prison with credit for the time he served. Meanwhile Palmer remained free pending appeal.

In January of 1981 the Indiana Supreme Court ordered Palmer to prison. Bontrager, found in "indirect criminal contempt," was fined $500 and received a suspended thirty-day prison sentence. A year later, Bontrager resigned from the bench for other causes. In an editorial, *The Goshen News* commended his decision: "Judges must set a perfect example in following man's law, which a majority of state legislators must feel isn't contrary to God's law." [2] He formed a Christian mediation service, later worked with the Christian Legal Society in Minnesota, and consulted with Charles Colson's Prison Fellowship Ministry.

Author Mark Umbreit notes that "Palmer was again in prison, not for the commission of a new crime, nor for violation of the conditions of probation. Despite having already served more than a year behind bars and having been reconciled with his victims, Palmer had to leave his wife and two children, to return to the cold steel bars of the Indiana prison system.

"Palmer himself had now become victimized by a criminal justice system that was intent on adhering to the precise letter of the law, while violating the spirit of that same law. He was being penalized for the courageous actions of a judge who placed his commitment to his religious faith above the precise technicalities of the state."

Palmer worked as a clerk in the prison and led a Bible study group with other prisoners. Later, he worked for the prison chaplain and with the Prison Fellowship Ministry. Palmer believed that without "his strong belief in Jesus Christ and his ministry of reconciliation, he would not have been able to endure the intense feelings of frustration, anger, and alienation that he was periodically confronted with."

Palmer's church, the Southside Fellowship in Elkhart, Indiana, organized to urge Governor Robert D. Orr for clemency. Palmer received a hearing in July 1982. Letters in support of Palmer from across the country were exhibited as defense. Testimony was also provided by Palmer's wife, the Southside Fellowship, and a representative of the organization that ran the VORP program. Even Randy Brown, Palmer's victim, testified on Palmer's behalf. Admitting his hesitancy about Palmer, he asserted "that Palmer had been punished enough, and it was now time for him to return to his family."

In November 1982, Palmer was granted clemency on condition that he serve six months as a prisoner in a community-based work-release center. "Finally, after having been reconciled with a number of his victims, having endured several periods of incarceration in both Indiana and Michigan (totaling more than two and one-half years), having endured the loneliness and alienation of being caged and removed from his family, and after years of advocacy on his behalf from various supporters throughout the country, Fred Palmer was a free man." Sadly, Palmer later separated from his wife and they eventually divorced. "His own family had now become secondary victims of the crime and punishment experienced by this troubled Vietnam veteran."

Umbreit asks:

> Was justice really served by pressing this case and reincarcerating Fred Palmer? Or, had justice already been served by the mere fact that victims were receiving repayment, were satisfied with the action of the court, and Palmer himself was, by any definition, rehabilitated?
>
> At a time when our nation's prison system is bulging and the cost of incarceration is skyrocketing, what is the sense of being so determined to incarcerate a nonviolent convicted criminal

like Fred Palmer? With Indiana's prison system 40 percent over capacity and under two federal court orders to reduce overcrowding, and with the clear need to have space available for more violent, repetitive criminals—why Palmer?

In responding to an offender like Palmer, does it make sound economic sense to require a punishment far more costly to the taxpaying public than the actual financial loss to his victims, while at the same time restricting his ability to further repay his victims?

The vindictiveness of the system when nothing practical could be gained shows that the justice system is intrinsically retributive.

The Fred Palmer story had all the makings of a successful example of alternative justice. Palmer did not get off with "cheap grace," but had to deal with his crimes and their consequences in real ways. His life was getting back on track. He experienced reconciliation on many levels: with God, with himself, within his family, with his victims, and with his community in that he was making a productive contribution to society.

Palmer won over his former enemies, the Browns and Yohns. Randy Yohn, a police officer, eventually became sheriff of the Elkhart County sheriff's department and the chairperson of the local board that supervises the Elkhart, Indiana, VORP. Although Palmer was honoring the spirit of the law ("fulfilling the law" as the apostle Paul might say), the state insisted on its retribution anyway: Palmer had to serve a mandatory sentence. State law insists on punishment, but God's laws strive for redemption.

Palmer's wife and children also suffered. There is something tragically wrong when state justice blatantly overrides the welfare of everyone involved: victim, offender, and community. We must conclude that often law does not serve God's priorities of restoration, redemption, and reconciliation.

Yet we can be grateful for those Christians who worked for restorative justice in Fred Palmer's situation. If not for Judge Bontrager and the others who intervened, Umbreit asks, would Palmer's victims have been more satisfied? Would they have been able to meet this young decorated war veteran, family man, and Christian who had done them wrong but was still a person struggling in his own way to make it in American society? Would the numerous questions and fears that these victims experienced from having the sanctity of their homes violated and their property stolen have been answered and expressed? With Palmer behind bars for ten to twenty years, would his victims have experienced a more intense sense of justice?

The Failure of Old Answers

This story raises serious questions about the "criminal justice" practiced in North America, questions that test basic assumptions of our society. In the last chapter we saw how the basic needs of victims are ignored in our criminal justice system. Now we see that offenders are also badly used in this system.

Most acknowledge that our criminal justice system is a mess. Newspapers decry a steady rise in crime. Television episodes depict hardened criminals avoiding prosecution by technical loopholes. Some programs search for "most wanted" criminals. As I write, many gubernatorial eligibles in the United States portray themselves as get-tough candidates who want to bring back or beef up the death penalty. One governor's election ads show him with enlarged photographs of murderers executed during his tenure. George Bush's 1988 presidential campaign benefited immeasurably from the commercials that exploited Willie Horton, a paroled offender who committed horrible crimes.

Victims complain of being abused by the system. Convicts periodically explode in rage and riot. Nothing seems to work. Some want to get "tough" on crime, even though toughness has never worked before. Some want to compassionately work for rehabilitation, but others fear such an approach might get out of hand.

We respond emotionally to crime issues, fearing for our security and worrying about our families' well-being. A common human response to pain and suffering is to isolate and avoid it. Maybe by keeping criminals in prisons we will not have to deal with them. Perhaps by taking pains to protect ourselves we will never be victims and not have to relate to other victims.

But these are not Christian options. Our neighbors—our brothers and sisters—are falling victim to a criminal justice system that harms both victims and offenders. We have no choice but to search for a better way.

An Alternative to Retribution

Howard Zehr has explored the differences between retributive justice and restorative justice. Retributive justice has more to do with punishment; restorative justice has more to do with redemption. We can look at his distinctions by applying them to Fred Palmer's case.

1. In retributive justice, **crime violates the state and its laws.** Crime is an offense against the state. (In the last chapter, we heard a prosecutor tell a victim: "You are not part of this case; you just happened to be the victims. This was an offense against the state, and that's how we handle it.") Thus Fred Palmer became the responsibility of the state once he was convicted of certain crimes. He was guilty of breaking a state law. Whether or not he violated the Browns, the Yohns, or his own family was immaterial. The affected community of victims is not included in the "due process."

In restorative justice, however, **crime violates people and relationships.** In this understanding we see that Palmer's offense was against other people, against their homes, against their sense of security, against their property. Crime is a breakdown of community, a breakdown that can only be restored by the community.

2. Retributive justice **focuses on determining blame and guilt in the past** (i.e., **did he/she do it?**). In investigations and prosecution, authorities wanted to decide whether Palmer had done the deed. They were not concerned with how Palmer's economic history and his experience as a soldier affected his deeds. They were not concerned about his family, people who were also directly victimized by this tragedy. They were not concerned about what action would be best for Palmer.

Restorative justice **aims to identify needs and obligation, with a future-oriented focus on problem solving** (i.e., **what**

should be done?). Even if a person is guilty, the question needs to be: Why did the person do this and how can we ensure that she or he will not do this again? Sending people to prison where they become hardened in antisocial aggression does not accomplish this.

Palmer needed ways to "make good" with his victims and answer to them rather than pay an anonymous debt to a faceless society.

3. In retributive justice, **the offender is pitted against the state in an adversarial relationship of "due process."** Court trials are not so much a careful investigation of the truth as a contest between lawyers (paid professional proxies). The contest is set up so that between the state and the accused, one must be a winner and the other a loser. Because of the high stakes involved, it is not always in an accused person's best interest to be forthrightly honest in court. (Lawyers often train clients in how to obscure the truth, rather than bring clarity.)

In restorative justice, **negotiation and exchange of information are done in ways that give victims and offenders central roles.** The insights of the victim-offender mediation made a crucial contribution to this process of bringing healing to both victims and offender. Restorative justice encourages the direct involvement and the forthright truth-telling of all parties.

4. In retributive justice, **doses of pain are measured out to punish, deter, and prevent future crimes.** Fred Palmer was sentenced to an automatic mandatory sentence. This was to punish his misdeed and to pay off his debt to society.

In restorative justice, **the priorities are restitution as a means of restoring both parties with the hope of reconciliation as the goal, so that insofar as possible things can be made right.** For Palmer, this meant hard work in dealing with his victims and seeking to make restitution. He might also have been required to deal with his wrongful ways of dealing with economic pressures.

5. In retributive justice, **rules and intentions outweigh outcomes: one side wins and the other loses.** Palmer was duly convicted of his crimes. In this process, the victim is ignored and a convicted offender merely receives punishment.

But restorative justice is **judged by the extent to which** responsibilities are assumed, needs are met, and healing (of individuals and relationships) is encouraged. These goals were being met by Palmer and those working with him. Both victims and offenders must be part of the process of restoration. But those positive accomplishments were undermined when the state insisted on a mandatory sentence.

"Justice is to be tested by the outcome, not the procedures, and it must come out with right relationships. Justice is a process of making things right." [3]

Throughout most of history (and in some countries today) justice has been seen as a community priority rather than a state monopoly. More importantly, biblical teachings point to redemption and restoration as a better goal than retribution. In the next two chapters we will turn to the Bible, our most important resource for understanding justice.

For Discussion

1. Carefully review Mark Umbreit's questions as found on pp. 20-22.

2. In what ways was Fred Palmer's case unusual? In what ways was it not unusual?

3. How does the Fred Palmer story illustrate the retributive nature of our criminal justice systems?

4. What are the restorative implications of Jesus' parable in Matthew 25:31-46? What might be the implications of Jesus' encounter with Zacchaeus (Luke 19:1-10)? Are there any implications in the fact that Jesus replaced one criminal (Barabbas) and was crucified between two criminals?

5. Are Jesus' responses to offenders restorative or retributive in Matthew 5:38-48 or Luke 6:27-36? How can Jesus' advice in John 8:7 affect our approach to criminal justice issues?

6. What are some of the problems with our criminal justice systems?

7. Why do we feel so deeply about crime issues? What are some of your fears and concerns?

8. Are you personally acquainted with offenders? How did they experience the criminal justice system? Did it help to restore the offenders? heal relationships?

9. What do you see as the most important differences between retributive and restorative justice? Is one more biblical than the other? In what ways?

10. Can justice be a combination of restoration and retribution?

11. Does Jesus' emphasis on restoration and redemption apply only between individuals or does it also apply to the state?

Aids to Reflection

In today's justice, all action is hierarchical, from the top down. The state acts on the offender, with the victim on the sidelines. Restorative justice would put victim and offender at the center, helping to decide what is to be done about what has happened. Thus the definition of accountability would change. Instead of "paying a debt to society" by experiencing punishment, accountability would mean understanding and taking responsibility for what has been done and taking action to make things right. Instead of owing an abstract debt to society, paid in an abstract way by experiencing punishment, the offender would owe a debt to the victim, to be repaid in a concrete way.

—Howard Zehr, *Retributive Justice, Restorative Justice.*

The trouble is that under our adversarial system of law an attorney's first concern is not with a witness's truthfulness or an accused person's guilt. The adversarial system is not about truth and justice (the words emblazoned on the statues that guard the entrance to the Supreme Court of Canada building) but about winning and losing. Osgoode Hall law professor Allan Hutchinson points out that a good lawyer who today argues with eloquence and conviction for one viewpoint on a matter of law could tomorrow argue in another courtroom with the same eloquence and conviction for the opposite view. Depending on the quality of the opposition, the leanings of the judge, and the availability of funds for an appeal process that could settle the issue decisively, the oscillating advocate could win on both days.

—Ivor Shapiro, "Devil's Advocate," *Saturday Night*, December 1989.

No matter how we try to rationalize or justify or sanitize the use of imprisonment, prison confinement is a destructive and irresponsible way to treat human beings, regardless who the human being is or what s/he has done that offends us. Prison takes away a person's dignity. Prison opens wounds. Prison prevents us from establishing more real and loving relationships. Prison legitimizes the barriers we have already built around our hearts, barriers that conveniently allow us to ignore the more unpleasant, uncomfortable aspects of one another's humanity. Prison keeps us blind to the fact that in every human person, no matter how broken, hardened, dominating or cruel, there is a spring of water waiting to flow forth.

—John Cole Vodicka of Alderson Hospitality House, West Virginia, in MCC's *Criminal Justice Network Newsletter*, July-September 1989.

Incarceration is perhaps the most obvious way in which we avoid the awareness of our own evil and guilt.

—Thomas R. Neufeld, *Guilt and Humanness*, Church Council on Justice and Corrections, 1976.

The criminal law system that we have promises us security against criminals. Does it follow through? No. It is not justice. You will remember one of the famous sayings in the Bible, in the New Testament, that a tree shall be judged by its fruit. An apple tree that produces apples is a real apple tree. An apple tree that does not produce apples is worthless and you throw it out into the fire. That is what the text says, and quite rightly so. A criminal law system that does not bring justice is like an apple tree that does not produce apples. The criminal law system does not produce justice and does not produce security. On the contrary, it provokes criminality: the prison system produces criminals, then throws them into society. The phrase "criminal justice" is an abomination. You should abolish it. It is nonsensical, absurd, and, religiously speaking, a forbidden expression.

—Herman Bianchi, *A Biblical Vision of Justice*, New Perspectives on Crime and Justice: Occasional Papers: Issue No. 2, MCC Office of Criminal Justice, 1984.

END NOTES

1 This story is adapted from Mark Umbreit, *Crime and Reconciliation*, (Nashville: Abingdon, 1985), pp. 21-34. Unless otherwise noted, all quotes are from Umbreit.

2 Quoted by Millard C. Lind, "Law in the Old Testament," in *Monotheism, Power, Justice: Collected Old Testament Essays* (Elkhart Ind.: Institute of Mennonite Studies, 1990), p. 76.

3 Howard Zehr, *Retributive Justice, Restorative Justice* (Mennonite Central Committee U.S. Office of Criminal Justice, Occasional Papers No. 4, September 1985), p. 11.

CHAPTER 3

From Eye for Eye to Steadfast Love

Justice in the Old Testament

Where Should Killers Go?

"Halfway house for killers coming here," the headline blared. When St. Leonard's House, a prison rehabilitation society, proposed a halfway house in Windsor for paroled murderers, the press went wild. "Lifers" in Canada serve up to twenty-five years in prison and are then on lifelong parole. Parole violations, even the breaking of a curfew, can mean an additional year or even years in prison.

Soon the newspaper reported that "angry and fearful Windsor residents burned up the telephone lines to City Hall" in response to the story. Two local men who happened to have the same name as the chair of the halfway house project were harassed by a barrage of phone calls opposing the project. Because of this proposal, a friend who teaches in a martial arts school was approached by two women who wanted to learn self-defense. A lead editorial advised against Windsor's becoming the "convicted murderer capital of Canada." A local columnist said this would make the city "a glorified garbage can for the nation's overcrowded penitentiaries."

One front page showed a large color photo of a woman weeping by a grave. "Nothing halfway about her rage," said the headline. She mourned the death of her mother who had been stabbed by a parolee. He was not a paroled lifer, he had no connection with St. Leonard's, and his crime would not make him a lifer. Yet this irrelevant story was used vehemently to attack the proposal.

The pictured woman was quoted as saying: "I drink until I pass out so I can sleep. The nights I don't drink I don't sleep. I wake up every morning and I wonder, 'Well, Kelly, do you commit suicide and go to hell or do you live long enough to see that idiot get out of jail and kill him and go to hell?' " Much was omitted and downplayed in the news. Buried near the end of the article, on the "continued" page, was the comment of another victim who favored halfway houses: "If they're going to get out, let's do it right so there isn't another victim, so there isn't another murder."

Given this publicity, I should not have been surprised (although I was) when some local church people opposed the proposed halfway house. Windsorites feared twenty lifers living in a supervised halfway house for up to three years. Yet two dozen paroled lifers already live in Windsor: a local halfway house accommodates a few of them for six months and others live in relatively unsupervised independence. Largely ignored was the fact that lifers have the lowest rate of recidivism; they are usually one-time offenders.

St. Leonard's successful programs and its extensive experience with prisons and convicts was not considered. In fact, St. Leonard's was not described at all. Never mentioned was the fact that its halfway house is a good neighbor: since its inception, an elementary school, senior citizens' apartments, and a YMCA have been built on the same block. Local headlines transferred frustrations about crime and the criminal justice system to St. Leonard's, an agency that seeks to alleviate problems within the criminal justice system.

Lifers are a given. Because of lengthy prison terms, they have massive problems after leaving prison. After long periods in violent, same-sex societies (prisons), they often do not know how to function on the outside. Vocational and interpersonal skills dwindle. The long term in prison usually fractures all outside relations: half of lifers receive no letters or visitors. During most of their time in prison, the government has no programs for them. (As part of the halfway house program, St.

Leonard's would begin working with lifers as soon as they were incarcerated.) Aside from the moral good of caring for offenders, St. Leonard's serves society's self-interest in providing supervised reintegration for Canada's most troubled convicts.

Does the Bible Mandate Revenge?

The tumultuous feelings surrounding the proposed halfway house reflect many concerns. Certainly there is a concern for justice, even when people are not always sure what is just. There is fear about the danger of having convicted felons in our community. There is outrage over the prospect that murderers might get off too easily. Such outrage often translates into a thirst for revenge.

Issues of justice and crime, victims and offenders, are of great concern in the Bible. Many people assume that the Bible advocates a hard and vengeful line toward offenders. While "eye for eye and tooth for tooth" is not the most important thing that the Bible has to say on these matters, it is probably the most well-known. Thus, in our study of the Old Testament, we must examine familiar calls for retribution and revenge.

There are many Old Testament laws that we no longer apply. For example, no one today recommends executing rebellious children as commanded in Deuteronomy 21:18-21, even though that law may have once served a legitimate function.

How then do we apply the Old Testament today? First, we must understand the context of Old Testament society and the purposes of its laws. Second, we must listen to the witness of the entire Bible, with the principles of the New Testament taking priority.

Reading the whole Bible witness, we will see that God was constantly moving his people, calling them to new depths and implications of justice. While God's people absorbed laws from the cultures around them, God's priorities fundamentally altered the applications and implications of those laws.

God's Justice Versus Society's Justice

Clarence Jordan shows how God steadily pushes each culture

and society beyond its comfort zones when working on issues of violence and crime. [1]

1. The most natural reaction to crime, sin, or offense is *unlimited retaliation*. From early on, this was the normal response. Cain's descendant, Lamech, made this fearful boast to his wives: "I have killed a man for wounding me, a young man for striking me. If Cain is avenged sevenfold, truly Lamech seventy-seven fold" (Genesis 4:23b-24). Here there was no due or just proportion between offense and retribution, only unlimited retaliation.

2. God responds to unlimited retaliation by commanding *limited retaliation*: "Whoever sheds the blood of a human, by a human shall that person's blood be shed; for in his own image God made humankind" (Genesis 9:6). That verse is often used to justify capital punishment, but it was intended as a limitation on vengeance.

John Howard Yoder notes that this death penalty "is clearly not so much a requirement as a limitation. It is spoken against the background of a story of corruption (Genesis 4 to 6) in which vengeance was the general pattern." [2] God was not ordering a law of revenge.

"Vengeance does not need to be commanded; it happens. It is the normal response of fallen humanity to any situation that calls forth hostility. And normally such vengeance is unlimited." [3]

Unlimited retaliation remains a temptation. Clarence Jordan points out that humanity has not outgrown this, "but has lapsed back into it with the invention of the atom bomb. This seems to be the principle that dominates the State Departments of most so-called civilized nations. You bomb us, we'll obliterate you. You bomb a little city, we will annihilate a whole nation. Unlimited, massive retaliation." [4]

"Eye for eye" laws (often called *lex talion*: Exodus 21:22-25; Leviticus 24:19-20; Deuteronomy 19:21) are familiar, but their importance is limited: they are mentioned only three times. Their purpose or spirit was to limit and restrain violence and vengeance; they did not command revenge. In fact, Israel's law code was the only one in the Ancient Near East that restricted "eye for eye" to the offender; other societies allowed retribution to be waged further afield, even against an offender's family. [5] To apply the spirit of the Old Testament's "eye for eye" laws today would be to limit and restrain violence.

Capital punishment laws were also severely restricted and restrained in their application: "there was a saying that a Sanhedrin which put one man to death in seven years might be called murderous. Rabbi Eliezer ben Azarya said that it (the Sanhedrin) would be called murderous if it executed one man in seventy years." [6] Cities of refuge (Exodus 21:12-14; Numbers 35:9-34; Deuteronomy 19:1-3) were another restriction and limitation on vengeance; "they allowed time for tempers to cool in order to work out a more positive resolution." [7] Nevertheless, such cities were primarily meant to protect the wrongly accused or those whose accidents resulted in death.

Thus God called people to a higher standard than surrounding peoples: *limited violence* rather than *unlimited violence*. "Get even, but no more. Do unto others as they do unto you." [8] While this was an improvement, it did not yet match God's ideal. His people were not allowed to rest easy here.

3. God's society cannot be built on violence, limited or unlimited. Thus God called the faithful beyond limited violence to *limited love* towards one's own people. "You shall not hate in your heart anyone of your kin. . . . You shall not take vengeance or bear a grudge against any of your people, but you shall love your neighbor as yourself: I am the Lord" (Leviticus 19:17-18).

Jordan writes: "The idea was that there had to be some limit to this love and goodwill business, and the proper place to draw the line was with your own race. In this way a man could have two standards of righteousness: one in dealing with his kinsmen and another in dealing with strangers." [9]

4. But God's directives point toward his goal of *unlimited love*. This is exemplified in the New Testament by Jesus. In contrast to Lamech's seventy-fold vengeance, Jesus recommends unlimited forgiveness, "seventy times seven" (Matthew 18:22, RSV). In contrast to limited retaliation, he says: "But I say to you, Do not resist one who is evil" (Matthew 5:39a, RSV) and rejects "an eye for an eye." In the Lord's Prayer, he

reminds us to pray: "Forgive us our sins, as we forgive those who have sinned against us" (Matthew 6:12). Revenge is abolished (Romans 12:17ff). Not do-unto-others-as-they-do-unto-you, but "do to others as you would have them do to you; for this is the law and the prophets" (Matthew 7:12). In contrast to limited love, Jesus commends unlimited love: "Love your enemies and pray for those who persecute you" (Matthew 5:44).

Jesus' teachings are based on "the law and the prophets" (Matthew 7:12). "Think not that I have come to abolish the law and the prophets; I have come not to abolish them but to fulfill them" (Matthew 5:17,RSV). Jesus saw something in the Old Testament that many overlook.

Justice in the Old Testament

At first God commended *limited retaliation* and then *limited love*. God's purpose was always to call people towards *unlimited love*, which was already beginning to be commended in the Old Testament.

When we read the Old Testament, we should not dwell only on vengeful texts. "One of the striking things about the way in which Jesus uses the Old Testament is the complete absence of the theme of vengeance in His references. On a number of occasions Jesus refers to a theme from an Old Testament prophet but stops short of the reference to vengeance (especially Isaiah 61, cf. Luke 4)." [10]

While Jesus eloquently advocates *unlimited love*, there are already suggestions of it in the Old Testament. For example, Hebrew laws were the only laws in the Ancient Near East that made special provisions for foreigners (Exodus 22:21; 23:9). [11] "The alien who resides with you shall be to you as the citizen among you; you shall love the alien as yourself, for you were aliens in the land of Egypt: I am the Lord your God" (Leviticus 19:34). All God's laws are based on Israel's experience of God as a redeemer and savior from slavery and oppression in a foreign land.

God often points back to the people's liberation from enslavement in Egypt. That salvation is the basis for biblical law and justice. Thus the Ten Commandments begin with this: "I am the Lord your God, who brought you out of the land of

Egypt, out of the house of slavery" (Exodus 20:2). No other Near Eastern laws began with emancipation from slavery. [12] God's actions in history produce laws that encourage God's people to act with the same kinds of redemptive justice.

The most important aspect of God's justice, law, and righteousness is rescuing and redeeming. Old Testament law strove for redemption rather than punishment. "God's righteousness is that he rescues people in need—in spite of their guilt. . . . No blindfolded justice here!" [13]

The purpose of God's justice was shalom: right-relationships personally and corporately, privately and publicly, economically and morally, between person and person and between persons and God. Shalom was rooted in God's way of dealing with Israel. Shalom is at the very core of God's hopes and intentions for humanity.

Biblically, then, acts that claim to be just are judged by whether or not they move towards God's redemptive shalom. "The test of justice in the biblical view is not whether the right rules are applied in the right way. Justice is tested by the outcome. The tree is tested by its fruit." [14]

With God, there is no dichotomy between mercy and justice. Biblical justice grows out of love. Such justice is in fact an act of love that seeks to make things right. Love and justice are not opposites, nor are they in conflict. Instead, love provides for a justice that seeks first to make right. [15]

Over and again, God responded to offense with mercy, seeking to restore offenders into right relationship with him. God responded to the first murder by protecting Cain against violence (Genesis 4:15). Cain deserved to die, but God was merciful. Although Moses and David were murderers, God chose to spare them. In the New Testament, Paul the murderer is likewise spared. "As I live, says the Lord God, I have no pleasure in the death of the wicked, but that the wicked turn from their ways and live; turn back, turn back from your evil ways; for why will you die, O house of Israel?" (Ezekiel 33:11).

Each time people rebel against God, God seeks to restore them—in spite of wilderness wanderings, in spite of choosing human kings, in spite of idolatry, in spite of military alliances, in spite of injustice and oppression. "The real story of the

Bible, from the Old Testament into the New, is this: God does not give up. It is precisely in this way that we are to imitate God, to be 'perfect': in indiscriminate love, in love that is undeserved, in forgiveness, in mercy." [16]

Sometimes we remember only God's anger and revenge in the Old Testament: "I the Lord your God am a jealous God, punishing children for the iniquity of parents, to the third and the fourth generation of those who reject me" (Exodus 20:5). Yet we forget the conclusion of that verse: "but showing steadfast love to the thousandth generation of those who love me and keep my commandments" (Exodus 20:6). While the third and fourth generations may feel God's zeal, thousands of generations (cf. Deuteronomy 20:6) enjoy God's steadfast love. God's loving mercy outstrips his wrath. "What god can compare with you: taking fault away, pardoning crime, not cherishing anger for ever but delighting in showing mercy?" (Micah 7:18, JB).

> Yahweh is tender and compassionate,
>   slow to anger, most loving;
> his indignation does not last for ever,
>   his resentment exists a short time only;
> he never treats us, never punishes us,
>   as our guilt and our sins deserve. (Psalm 103:8-10, JB)

For Discussion

1. Given what the Old Testament says about justice, consider how biblical Christians would respond to the issue of St. Leonard's halfway house. How did the news stories emphasize retribution, revenge, and fear? Where and in what ways could a Christian emphasize restoration and reconciliation?

2. How might the church model itself after Cities of Refuge? (Exodus 21:12-14; Numbers 35:9-34; Deuteronomy 19:1-3). A place for calm discussion of highly emotional issues? A place to examine both sides of the issue with the hopes of mitigating retribution and promoting costly reconciliation? Could halfway houses themselves be seen as descendants of such sanctuary cities?

3. How do limited and unlimited retaliation and love fit here? Presumably, lifers committed unlimited retaliation

against their victims. Is life imprisonment limited or unlimited vengeance? How do those who oppose the halfway house alternative perpetuate unlimited vengeance? How can Christians promote unlimited love in such difficult circumstances?

4. How might God the "righteous-rescuing judge" respond to paroled lifers? How does God respond with mercy to offense? How might we respond to offenders?

5. Is it reasonable to assume that most lifers are poor? How does God respond to the poor and vulnerable? How does God respond to those whose own sin has made them poor and vulnerable?

6. Was the newspaper's outrage in the interest of shalom? Was it interested in the well-being of offenders, victims, or the community? Was it exploiting an emotional issue without clarifying and exploring?

7. How might Christians have approached the issue of St. Leonard's halfway house for lifers? What might you or your pastor have done?

8. What were your main impressions of the Old Testament's teachings on justice before you read this chapter? Did you encounter any surprises here?

9. Why did God shift emphasis from limited retaliation to limited love to unlimited love and forgiveness? Was God inconsistent? Why or why not? Which is to be our main emphasis?

Aids to Reflection

Our first—and often only—response after guilt has been established is to deliver pain as punishment. Once delivered, the process of justice has ended. When punishment occurs in covenant justice, however, it is not usually the end but the means toward ultimate restoration. Moreover, punishment is primarily God's business. The primary focus of biblical justice is to make things right, to build shalom, by acting in aid of those in need.

Today the test of justice often is whether the proper procedures have been followed. Biblical . . . justice is measured by the substance, by the outcome, by its fruits. Does the outcome work to make things right? Are things being made right for the poor and the least powerful, the least "deserving"? Biblical justice focuses on right relationships, not right rules.

Our legal system defines offenses as violations of rules, of laws. We define the state as the victim. In biblical terms, however, wrongdoing is not a contravention of rules but a violation of right relationships. People and relationships, not rules or governments or even a moral order, are the victims.

—Howard Zehr, *Changing Lenses.*

Justice is far more than fair treatment and due process. It is also more than vindication of those who have been wronged and punishment of the wrongdoer. The full meaning of justice is to establish once again the shalom that existed before the offense. Justice is active and relational and it is redemptive in its intent.

—Daniel W. Van Ness, *Crime and its Victims.*

Biblical writers reject the idea that man should ever execute vengeance on his fellowman. For a cardinal point in both Hebrew and Christian faith is that only God can execute judgment or vengeance and that whenever man avenges a wrong he arrogates to himself a place which only God can take.

—William Klassen, *Release to Those in Prison.*

Thus when in the Sermon on the Mount or in Romans 12, *all* vengeance is declared illegitimate for the Christian, or when Jesus' own death is seen in the New Testament as a proclamation of forgiveness, this is another step in the direction already taken by Genesis 9 and Exodus 21. Vengeance was never God's highest intent for men's relations with one another; permitting it within the limits of justice, i.e., of equivalent injury was never really His purpose. What God always wanted to do with evil, and what He wants men today to do with it is to swallow it up, drown it in the bottomless sea of His crucified love.

—John Howard Yoder, *Capital Punishment.*

END NOTES

1   The analysis of unlimited vengeance, limited vengeance, limited love, and unlimited love is from Clarence Jordan, *Sermon on the Mount*, Revised Edition (Valley Forge: Judson Press, 1952), pp. 63-71.

2   John Howard Yoder, *The Christian and Capital Punishment* (Newton: Faith and Life Press, 1961), p. 6.

3   Yoder, *The Christian and Capital Punishment*, p. 6.

4   Clarence Jordan, *Substance of Faith*, ed. Dallas Lee (New York: Association Press, 1972), p. 70.

5   M. Greenberg, "Crimes and Punishments," in *Interpreter's Dictionary of the Bible*, vol. 1 (Nashville: Abingdon, 1962), p. 734.

6   William Barclay as quoted in *Capital Punishment Study Guide* (Victim Offender Ministries, MCC Canada, 1987), p. 8.

7   Mark Umbreit, *Crime and Reconciliation* (Nashville: Abingdon, 1985), p. 73.

8   Jordan, *Sermon on the Mount*, p. 65.

9   Jordan, *Sermon on the Mount*, pp. 65-66

10   William Klassen, *Release to Those in Prison* (Scottdale: Herald Press, 1977), p. 26.

11   Millard C. Lind, "Law in the Old Testament," in *Monotheism, Power, Justice: Collected Old Testament Essays* (Elkhart, Ind.: Institute of Mennonite Studies, 1990), p. 67.

12   Hans Jochen Boecker, *Law and the Administration of Justice in the Old Testament and Ancient East*, trans. Jeremy Moisier (Minneapolis: Augsburg Publishing House, 1980), p. 156.

13   Carl Graesser, Jr., "Righteousness, Human and Divine," *Currents in Theology and Ministry*, 10, 1983, p. 140.

14   Howard Zehr, *Changing Lenses* (Scottdale: Herald Press, 1990), p. 140.

15   Zehr, *Changing Lenses*, p. 139.

16   Zehr, *Changing Lenses*, p. 146.

CHAPTER 4

A Wideness in God's Mercy
Justice in the New Testament

Costly Errors, Costly Reconciliation

The following story by Clare Bauman appeared the in *Menno-nite Reporter*, January 8, 1990.

"You are in big trouble. At least one dead and several injured." Those were the words of the police officer as he arrested me.

I had been drinking in the afternoon and caused an accident on the way home, close to Elmira, Ontario, on Good Friday, 1988. I fell asleep at the wheel and ran into the Elmer Weber family in their horse-drawn buggy.

I killed seven-month-old Erla Weber. Her mother and sister were injured, the whole family was emotionally scarred and I was charged with impaired driving causing death.

After the accident I went through a time of terrible emotional turmoil. I decided I must go and see the parents of the little girl I had killed. It was the hardest thing I have ever done but I knew I could not live with myself if I did not go.

On Easter Sunday morning my wife and I went to the Weber home. We were warmly received by Elmer's parents; Elmer was with his wife Elsie at the Listowel Hospital. Before we left they asked us if we wanted to view the body, which we did.

When we got to the hospital we met Elmer and Elsie (who was walking with the aid of a walker) in the hall. I was very nervous and could not contain my tears.

Elmer noticed me and asked, "Are you Clare?" When I was able to find words, I said to Elmer, "I hope that you can forgive me, some day."

His reply was, "We have forgiven you already."

I will be forever grateful that they gave me their hand of love and not a fist of hate when I came to ask their forgiveness. They were mourning the loss of a child but could still smile through the tears and show concern for me.

The following Tuesday I attended the funeral for Erla. The Old Order Mennonite minister was redemptive and did not condemn. He encouraged the family and congregation to pray for me.

A month later my wife and I had a nice visit with the Weber family in their home. The response of the children was very touching. Their little daughter was very playful, sharing her toys with my wife. I visited Elmer in his furniture shop where his son showed me a miniature roll-top desk he had made.

In this and subsequent visits Elmer and Elsie were always concerned for me and what I had yet to face—court and imprisonment

Eight months and one day after the accident, I appeared in court for sentencing. The Webers had said from the beginning that they did not want to see me go to jail, but I knew that justice would not be served otherwise.

I told my lawyer that I could not put Mr. Weber through the ordeal of testifying at a trial. I insisted on pleading guilty. I was sentenced to three years in a federal prison.

I knew no length of sentence would make up for the loss felt by the Weber family and was willing to accept the sentence imposed by the court.

The next six or seven weeks were difficult ones. This was a time of transition from Waterloo Detention Centre to the maximum security Millhaven institution. Since this was the Christmas season, life for me was especially depressing.

One thing that brightened these weeks, besides the visits from my wife and family, was the letters from the Webers and the two visits that Elmer made while I was at Waterloo Detention Centre.

This was also the time I began a serious study of God's Word and a closer walk with the Lord, which gave me strength to face each new day. The following summer the Weber family also visited me in Kingston.

When I got my first weekend pass, Elmer called me at my home. I was not permitted to contact the victim's family according to the conditions of my pass, but they could contact me.

Relationships with my family improved. I learned that my home community was inquiring about me. My church had a note in the bulletin requesting prayer for me.

I continue to serve my sentence but am grateful for the freedom God has brought to my life. I am free from alcohol and by the grace of God I can overcome all the devil's temptations.

For a long time I found it hard to accept the forgiveness of God. And I had a hard time forgiving myself. I can never forget what I did: it cost the life of little Erla to change mine.

I thank God for giving the Webers the will to forgive me. I thank God for all the wonderful people who have helped me through this, including Jake Thiessen, Gary Knarr, my family and in-laws, friends and especially my wife, Elmeda.

I write this in the hope that all who read it will be challenged to exercise Christ's forgiveness in their lives, and tear down the walls of bitterness and strife that the Evil One would build in our lives.

"Forgive us our trespasses, as we forgive those who trespass against us."

The Webers and indeed Clare Bauman are exceptional people. We do not expect to encounter victims so able to forgive and so long-suffering in their outreach to an offender. Nor do we anticipate offenders to repent so promptly. While this may all seem quite unusual to us, by biblical standards it is normal. We are expected to act no differently.

Whatever Happened to Just Desserts?

We expect people to get what they deserve and what they deserve is based on what they do. That's only common sense. But Jesus acted outrageously on the question of just desserts. This is clear in his parable of the laborers in the vineyard (Matthew 20:1-17). Those who began work early and those who began work late all received exactly the same wage!

In the previous chapter, we saw that Jesus moved beyond limited love to *unlimited love* by commending *unlimited forgiveness* and rejecting revenge. This principle obviously applies to how we deal with offenders.

Because the church discipline recommended in Matthew 18 has sometimes been applied harshly, we may see it negatively. However, the thrust of the passage is reconciliation and restoration, trying to regain your Christian brother or sister (Matthew 18:15). Jesus recommends that one who is continually unrepentant be treated "as a gentile and a tax collector." What does he mean? Jesus advises not *condemnation* here but *evangelization*. If someone violates the fellowship we should try to win him or her back.

Jesus had a special concern for outsiders and recommends the same to us. Fallen-away siblings are to be wooed again with the gospel of Christ, so that they might hopefully reenter God's fold. Thus this passage is directly connected to what follows in Matthew 18:21-35, where Jesus teaches unlimited forgiveness. Ultimately, it is not sinners who are condemned, but those who refuse forgiveness to offenders. "So my heavenly Father will also do to every one of you, if you do not forgive your brother or sister from your heart" (Matthew 18:35; cf. 6:14).

Jesus goes further, of course, in recommending that we love even our enemies (Matthew 5:38ff.).

> If we think these words are preposterous, they were no less so for Jesus' original audience. For his hearers, "enemies" were Roman occupation forces. Or "enemies" were bandits who would sweep down from the hills to pillage and burn. In other words: "enemies" are those who injure or threaten injury. [1]

Jesus was talking about violent offenders who caused terrible harm. Jesus was not being naive, sentimental, idealistic, or romantic with this outrageous advice: "Jesus does not do away with the notion of 'enemies.' Enemies are clearly those who threaten us, and Jesus' comments neither camouflage nor sentimentalize that fact." [2]

We all benefit from God's grace: rewards and salvation are not on the basis of merit or good deeds. Whenever the "righteous" are tempted to exclude or condemn "offenders," then the "righteous" are rebuked and the "offenders" invited, affirmed, embraced, and welcomed (e.g., Matthew 20:11-16; Luke 7:39-50; 15:25-32; 18:9-14; John 8:7-11). "Or do you begrudge my generosity?" (Matthew 20:15b, RSV).

God's mercy has nothing to do with our innate goodness. It is freely offered and freely given. "But now, *apart from law*, the righteousness of God has been disclosed. . . . For there is no distinction, since all have sinned and fall short of the glory of God; they are now justified by his grace as a gift, through the redemption that is in Christ Jesus" (Romans 3:21-24). In his song, "In the Falling Dark," Bruce Cockburn notes: "Don't you know that from the first to the last we're all one in the gift of Grace!" God does not meet our needs on the basis of what we do, but because of his love for us. God lovingly ministers to our needs, not meting out on the basis of our merits.

In Mark 5, Jesus encounters a demoniac in the country of the Gerasenes. This man was rejected and cut off from society, he had an "unclean spirit" and "lived among the tombs." Note his symbolic resemblance to convicted criminals in our society. Others tried to control him but could not: "for he had often been restrained with shackles and chains, but the chains he wrenched apart, and the shackles he broke in pieces" (v. 4). This dangerous man was bent on self-destruction, "bruising himself with stones." Jesus freed the man and did not bind him. He did not "subdue" the demoniac, but he could liberate him. The deliverance of this despised man is an example that calls us to similar action.

Jesus had an affinity for unclean sinners, criminals, prostitutes, tax collectors. In Luke 7, a sinful woman anointed Jesus' feet. A Pharisee was horrified that Jesus was physically touched by such a sinner, but Jesus was moved. He told a parable and concluded: "Therefore, I tell you, her sins, which were many, have been forgiven; hence she has shown great love. But the one to whom little is forgiven, loves little" (v. 47). Jesus' mercy applies in such a way that the greater the sinner the greater the forgiveness and mercy.

In Luke 19, Jesus attends a party with Zacchaeus. "All who saw it began to grumble and said, 'He has gone to be the guest of one who is a sinner' " (v. 7). They were content to condemn Zacchaeus from afar and to have nothing to do with him. But Jesus' direct contact resulted in Zacchaeus's repentance and his promise to make restitution to his victims: "Look, half of my possessions, Lord, I will give to the poor; and if I have defrauded anyone of anything, I will pay back four times as much" (v. 8). Jesus was delighted: "For the Son of Man came to seek out and to save the lost" (v. 10).

Jesus' attitude towards crime is further highlighted in the scandalous story found in John 8. A woman was caught in adultery and brought before Jesus. There is no doubt about her guilt. (Note the bias of this process of "justice" however: it takes at least two people to commit adultery but one of-fender—the male—is not presented for judgment.)

Jesus refused to condemn the woman to the death she de-served according to the law. "Let anyone among you who is without sin be the first to throw a stone at her" (v. 7). If we take this principle literally we cannot be part of a criminal justice system that judges others. "We dare not leave matters of jus-tice to the unjust courts, courts which do not accept the gospel as the norm and foundation for justice." [3] Jesus sets the woman free with a parting recommendation: "Neither do I condemn you. Go your way, and from now on do not sin again" (v. 11). She was freed with his invitation, advised to sin no more, but he imposes no condition on her release!

Jesus was not easy on offenders, he did not offer them "cheap grace." New Testament scholar Thomas Yoder Neufeld writes:

> And yet, there is never any evidence that Jesus in any way minimized [sinners'] offences. On the contrary, there are re-peated stories in which people who encountered Jesus (Zac-chaeus, the woman at the well, etc.) felt *exposed* and *confronted* by his presence. The only factor which can account for the strange combination of confrontation and exposure on the one hand and hospitality on the other, is Jesus' love and forgiveness. Jesus extended mercy and forgiveness, neither of which side-stepped the issue of sin, of offence, of crime. On the contrary, to offer forgiveness presupposes that there has been a real offence and the normal course of events would call for retribution and punishment. Forgiveness, further, presupposes that the offence was done by someone who is responsible for that action, who could have done differently, who has acted to break the relation-ship of solidarity upon which the fabric of human community depends. [4]

Thus Yoder Neufeld concludes: "Forgiveness takes sin and the sinner with the same utter seriousness as does wrath, venge-ance, and retribution." [5]

Jesus was not only an advocate on behalf of offenders. He became a victim himself when the powers-that-be accused him of being an offender. When he was arrested, one disciple tried to defend him, wounding a slave, but Jesus healed the wound of his enemy. He was crucified in the place of Barabbas, a murdering insurrectionist (Luke 23:18-25), symbolizing his substitution for all sinners and offenders. He was crucified between two criminals and figured in the saving conversion of one of them (Luke 23:33-43). Even as he suffered, he sought the reconciliation of others. Meanwhile, he went so far as to forgive all those who crucified him. "Father, forgive them; for they do not know what they are doing" (Luke 23:34).

The State and the Sword

Since we are trying to understand what the New Testament has to teach us about criminal justice, we must understand the role of government here. Some use Romans 13 to suggest that the state has the right to retribution, especially in areas of criminal justice; "for the authority does not bear the sword in vain!" (13:4b).

Note several things about this passage.

1. This does not give Christians the right to be agents of the state's wrath. Thus I am part of a tradition that recognizes our Christian obligation to conscientiously object to war.

2. The small passage in Romans 13:1-7 that deals with the state is embraced by a larger unit, Romans 12—13, which indicates that the highest ethical standards by which we live are nonconformity, forgiveness, and love. "Love does no wrong to a neighbor; therefore love is the fulfilling of the law" (13:10). Christians concerned about law and order need to grapple with God's understanding of law (see the next chapter).

3. While the state is intended to be God's servant, the Bible is clear that the state often violates God's will. We cannot assume that whatever the state does is what God wants. "There is a very strong strand of Gospel teaching which sees secular government as the province of the sovereignty of Satan." [6]

4. The "sword" in Romans 13 does not refer to the state

killing either in war or capital punishment. It was a dagger (not a weapon of war) that symbolized judicial authority. [7]

5. Our understandings of right and wrong, justice and law, offenders and victims cannot be ordered by the priorities of the state but fall under God's sovereignty and directives.

Be Reconciled to God

Second Corinthians 5:16—6:2 reflects some important themes of the gospel. Paul urges readers to live as reconciliation ambassadors. "In effect, this is an appeal to acknowledge the presence of 'a new creation' (5:17), and to allow that new creation to 'make a difference' in one's life. . . ." [8] Paul is both describing our reconciled status before God and urging us to live in this reality (5:19; 6:1-2).

Many Bible versions (RSV, NIV, NAB) translate the phrase "a new creation" personally and individually: "he is a new creation." But Paul's implications go beyond the personal and individual. "In fact, for him the 'new creation' amounts to a replacement of the old world: God did not simply 'recreate man.' " [9] The latter half of the verse (17b) means "a new order has already begun" (NEB) or "the new [creation] is here" (JB). The implications are phenomenal. This "makes clear that God's saving act in the death of Christ *embraces the whole world*." [10]

God accomplishes the reconciliation. Some suggest that Jesus' death was a way to reconcile us to God, as if God the Father is a cruel judge who needs to be placated by a blood sacrifice. But this is not Christ, the Defense Attorney, trying to win over God, the Hanging Judge. Rather, they work together in reconciling us. Too often, our understanding of what God did for us (justification, atonement) is compared to our criminal justice system. God does not practice retribution. God does not judge or punish as we deserve.

Romans 5:6ff. is closely related. We were weak, ungodly, sinners. Paul exclaims: "Indeed, rarely will anyone die for a righteous person. . . . But God proves his love for us in that while we still were sinners Christ died for us." Later, he goes even further: "While we were enemies we were reconciled to God." Before God, we are enemies, criminals, and offenders but God reverses our status. (In Matthew 5:38 ff., Jesus commends us to follow God's example here and love our enemies too.) God's atoning justification cannot compare to our criminal justice system.

Second Corinthians 5 is more powerful when considered within the context of Paul's letter. By the time 2 Corinthians was written, Paul had experienced imprisonment and death threats (1:8-10). The Corinthian church was plagued by problems: certain teachers and missionaries had challenged Paul's authority. Paul visited the congregation and suffered humiliation at the hand of these outsiders (2:5; 7:12; 12:14, 21; 13:1). Paul's emphasis on reconciliation is more striking in light of the rift he was experiencing with the congregation.

Paul writes from the context of suffering. He has experienced imprisonment, death threats, humiliation, and the prospect of failure in this church planting. He deals with hostility and division, desperately trying to keep the church together. That adds to the pathos of 5:15—6:2. His struggle for reconciliation is an attempt to avert tragedy. His suffering enhances his appreciation for how Christ works through suffering.

Paul appeals for Corinthian Christians to be reconciled both to God and to each other. He calls them to reflect the reconciliation reality in life, community, and deed. We are to be God's ministers, workers, ambassadors in proclaiming the message of God's reconciliation.

Will D. Campbell, the noteworthy author of *Brother to a Dragonfly* and committed civil rights activist, is greatly inspired by this 2 Corinthians 5 text. It is central to his life and work and is alluded to in a number of his books. Thus he calls for a church where enemies—including, for example, both racists and civil rights activists—can be together, learning to respect and embrace each other. In writing on the problems of the South, he calls Christians to minister reconciliation there, just as Paul ministered reconciliation in the troubled church of Corinth and just as we today are surely called to minister reconciliation in the breach between victims and offenders.

We have often noted that criminal justice issues provoke a lot of fears within us. We know our instinctive reaction to crime issues is to hate and seek revenge. Yet the New Testament challenges us to a more difficult, but ultimately better way. Jesus taught us that God loves us on the basis of our needs, not on the basis of our deeds. If we want to honor the New Testament's guidelines, then we will learn to love offenders, even when we find offenders unlovable.

For Discussion

1. Clare Bauman was not allowed to initiate contact with the family of victims after his conviction. Why would the courts make such a recommendation? How does this hinder restoration and reconciliation? When should exceptions be made to such rules?

2. How does Jesus respond to offenders in Luke 7:36-50; Luke 19:1-10; John 7:53—8:11? What implications does this have for our dealings with offenders?

3. What is taught about just desserts in the following passages: Matthew 20:1-16; Luke 15:11-32; Romans 3:21-26? Are we expected to act similarly?

4. Did the opening story seem realistic or exceptional? In 1990 in Canada, for the first time, an intoxicated driver received a life sentence. What is your response to such a sentence?

5. Does 2 Corinthians 5 seem a good summary of New Testament theology? of the gospel? Why or why not? If so, in what ways?

6. Does Jesus reconcile us to a difficult and angry God? Who does the work of reconciliation? What implications does this have for the way we treat offenders?

7. What circumstances make Paul's call for reconciliation in 2 Corinthians 5 so powerful and poignant?

8. What role might restitution play in processes of restoration and reconciliation?

9. How do Jesus and Paul advance (rather than contradict) themes that we encountered in the Old Testament?

10. How did Jesus' forgiveness work? Do you think it was effective?

11. How does Jesus identify with both victims and offenders?

12. What should the state's role be in the administration of justice? Can we expect it to live up to Jesus' restorative ideals?

Aids to Reflection

God is not said to *create* or *institute* or *ordain* the powers that be, but only to *order* them, to put them in order, sovereignly to tell them where they belong, what is their place. It is not as if there was a time when there was no government and then God made government through a new creative intervention; there has been hierarchy and authority and power since human society existed. Its exercise has involved domination, disrespect for human dignity, and real or potential violence ever since sin has existed. Nor is it that in his ordering of it he specifically, morally approves of what a government does. The sergeant does not produce the soldiers he drills, the librarian does not create nor approve of the book he catalogs and shelves. Likewise God does not take the responsibility for the existence of the rebellious "powers that be" or for their shape or identity; they already are. What the text says is that he orders them, brings them into line, that by his permissive government he lines them up with his purpose.

This is true of all governments. It is a statement both *de facto* and *de jure*. It applies to the governments of dictators and tyrants as well as to constitutional democracies. It would in fact apply just as well to the government of a bandit or a war lord, to the extent to which such would exercise real sovereign control.

—John Howard Yoder, *The Politics of Jesus*.

Thus we see that the grace of God is meant to be comforting, but it may be discomforting as well. It demands that we receive it as grace, remember it as grace, and grant to others equal access. No one, of course, has an earned "right" to grace, and so we are all on the same slippery footing when it comes to our standing before God. When we resent God's generosity to others, we undermine and refuse the grace that comes to us. We must judge others as we have been judged, we must forgive as we have been forgiven, and we must love as we have been loved. Thus we show ourselves to be the children

of grace rather than the children of arrogance.
—Clarence Jordan and Bill Lane Doulos, *Cotton Patch Parables of Liberation.*

The stance Jesus calls us to presupposes a deep and courageous faith in a God who is present and active in the midst of our relationships. The call to love the enemy, to forgive the offender does not come to us because it makes good practical sense, however true that might be in certain circumstances. It comes because we, as followers of Jesus, know ourselves to have been surprised by an undeserved forgiveness, and as such have in truth been called to nothing less vis-a-vis those who trespass against us. In this sense our task as forgivers is fundamentally evangelistic. However practical and creative the outworking of that forgiveness might be, the fundamental orientation does not arise out of pragmatism but out of a grateful, worshipful response of obedience to the call to imitate Jesus.
—Thomas R. Yoder Neufeld, "Forgiveness and the Dangerous Few: The Biblical Basis." Address to the Christian Council for Reconciliation, Montreal, November 18, 1983.

We need the presence of others for support and strength to exercise the courage and creativity of love when the time comes. We need others to remind us of the word of love when fear and hate and the desire for vengeance threaten to overtake us. We need others perhaps even to speak the word of forgiveness for us, when we ourselves are emotionally and spiritually incapable of it. To be asked to forgive, then, does not mean that one is left alone with that. We forgive as members of the body of the forgiving Christ. In short, to speak meaningfully of forgiveness in real human histories demands God's presence most especially as it resides in and expresses itself in the caring and believing community.
—Thomas R. Yoder Neufeld, "Forgiveness and the Dangerous Few: The Biblical Basis." Address to the Christian Council for Reconciliation, Montreal, November 18, 1983.

END NOTES

1 Thomas R. Yoder Neufeld, "Forgiveness and the Dangerous Few: The Biblical Basis." Address to the Christian Council for Reconciliation, Montreal, November 18, 1983, p. 4.

2 Yoder Neufeld, p. 4.

3 Millard C. Lind, "The Transformation of Justice," in *Monotheism, Power, Justice: Collected Old Testament Essays* (Elkhart, Ind.: Institute of Mennonite Studies, 1990), p. 94.

4 Emphasis added. Yoder Neufeld, p. 3.

5 Yoder Neufeld, p. 9.

6 John Howard Yoder, *The Politics of Jesus* (Grand Rapids: Eerdmans, 1972), p. 195.

7 Yoder, p. 206.

8 Victor Paul Furnish, *II Corinthians* (Garden City: Doubleday & Company, Inc., 1984), p. 350.

9 Hans Dieter Betz, *Galatians* (Philadelphia: Fortress, 1979), p. 320.

10 Emphasis added. Gunther Bornkamm, *Paul*, trans. D. M. G. Stalker (New York: Harper & Row, 1969), p. 141.

Chapter 5

What's So Good About Blind Justice?

The Purpose of Law

Just the Facts, Ma'am

Wayne Northey, who works with Victim Offender Ministries for Mennonite Central Committee Canada, tells of an incident that happened a decade ago:

I happened to be in court one day, and witnessed a not-so-unusual case. A man had been charged with assault causing bodily harm. He had not hired a lawyer. Rather, he appeared on his own behalf.

He was a big, muscular, good-looking man. He called his mother and sister in turn as witnesses. The facts of the situation leading up to his assault emerged. He was visiting his sister's apartment. A girlfriend of his sister came running over to that apartment. She was in a nightgown, bleeding, and obviously very upset. She explained that her father had been beating her up. So she fled the short distance to her girlfriend's apartment in search of protection.

Shortly afterwards, the father appeared. He knocked at the door and the brother answered. The father demanded that his daughter return home. The brother explained that she did not wish to, and that the father had no right beating on her and no right insisting upon her return.

The father tried to push his way into the apartment and force his daughter to go with him. The young man blocked his attempt. In the struggle, he hit the father on the jaw. The father's jaw was broken.

At that point the father left.

It was evident that the story as told fairly represented the events leading up to the assault.

The judge ignored every detail in the story but the actual matter of the offense. "Did you, or did you not," the judge intoned, "strike the complainant upon the jaw?"

"Yes, your Honor, but . . ."

"Then I find you guilty as charged and will sentence you."

The accused had never before had criminal charges against him. He staggered in disbelief at the swiftness with which his entire line of defense had been simply dismissed as irrelevant to the case.

The judge and the accused had different concepts of justice. The judge was only concerned about the rules governing the procedure. The rules dictated his course of action without any concern for the human story behind the events. Justice was blindfolded and therefore blind to the human needs of the case.

The law was applied, but justice was not served.

The Letter or the Spirit of the Law?

In our culture we see laws as a rigid, unbending set of rules that can be objectively and equally imposed in any situation. In fact, when laws are objectively imposed we believe that justice is done for "justice is blind." We also see Old Testament laws as a negative list of thou-shalt-nots. Thinking of the tablets Moses carried from the mountaintop, we may think of law as "carved in stone."

> We tend to interpret such law [as the Ten Commandments] from the perspective of our own law so we see them primarily as imperatives, prohibitions: "You must do this or else." But this law can be read in the future indicative. The Ten Commandments, like much biblical law, are like invitations, promises: "If you are really living as you should be, this is what life will be like. You will not kill. You will not steal." The Ten Commandments—and indeed the whole Torah—are intended as a pattern for living in covenant, in shalom. [1]

Israelite laws were given as teaching, preaching, advice and recommendations. [2] In fact, *torah* means teaching. When we understand law in this way, living well together becomes more important than enforcing rules, and we can lovingly invite others to live within God's redemptive community.

In Hebrew society, laws were not coldly imposed by an objective and impartial judge. "Given our understanding of the rigidity and finality of law, we are often amazed at the way the Israelites questioned and debated the law. But laws were to be used in teaching moral principle. Moreover they were starting points for discussion, for people were supposed to talk about the law." [3]

Laws were "wise indications" that helped point the way. [4] In other cultures, law was eternal and unchangeable, but Old Testament laws were uniquely flexible as they aimed for mercy, forgiveness, and shalom. [5] The best application of laws moves towards God's longed-for restoration, reconciliation, and redemption.

Later, when people got too caught up in the formality of rules, Jesus and Paul pointed out that the spirit of the law was more important than the letter: "for the letter kills, but the Spirit gives life" (2 Corinthians 3:6b). Thus when Jesus was confronted by the letter of the law that demanded a woman's death (John 8:4, 5), he did not coldly apply the verdict. Rather, he initiated a discussion of the principles behind the law: "Let anyone among you who is without sin be the first to throw a stone at her" (John 8:7). Elsewhere (Mark 2:23—3:6) he justified breaking Sabbath laws—also punishable by death—to uphold their underlying purpose.

The judge in our opening story missed the spirit, intent, and purpose of biblical law. He coldly applied the law, ignored the extenuating circumstances, and inflicted a punishment.

Justice: Retribution or Distribution?

The Bible's view of justice is different than society's view in other important ways. We tend to divide law into categories: civil and criminal, religious and secular, retributive and distributive. Biblical laws lump together all manner of concerns that we separate: family, agriculture, crime, social relations. God's view of justice affects all of life and all relations. Therefore the Bible does not distinguish between retributive and distributive justice. Retributive justice is "criminal law," concerned with meting out punishment. Distributive justice is "social justice," concerned with the economic arrangements of society: how resources and assets are allocated.

Once I was sent as a writer on an all-expenses-paid assignment in Philadelphia to attend a workshop on "restorative justice." I was embarrassed to find that I was put up in a hotel suite that had more square footage than my own home's first floor. Meanwhile, in the city I saw hungry and homeless men sleeping on grates in the street, trying to keep warm in the steam. I felt uneasy about my luxurious surroundings. While the workshop organizers promoted "restorative justice," they seemed unaware that they were participating in distributive injustice by choosing extravagant accommodations for the conference while basic human needs went unmet around them.

Two young Canadian Mennonites ventured across the river to Detroit. While there, they were robbed and one was shot in the leg. They found a police officer and made out a report. But when they went to the hospital emergency room, they were turned away. With no wallet and no credit cards, they could not prove they were able to pay for treatment. A police officer escorted them over the border and back to Canada where socialized medicine makes a small contribution to distributive justice. In Detroit, the "powers that be" were willing to engage in retributive justice (filing a police report and possibly investigating the crime). But this was fragmented justice: the wound was not cared for and health care was not available. Biblical justice is more holistic than Detroit's justice.

God is not only concerned about what we narrowly consider crime. "Injustice of any kind, in any sphere, is contrary to shalom. The acts of the one who oppresses are as serious as those of the one who assaults or robs." [6] In fact, God shows a special priority for the poor and oppressed. God's justice is biased towards the needy and the weak. Again and again, the Bible offers comfort to the poor, warnings to the rich, protection to the vulnerable, and judgment to oppressors.

For the poor who are exploited the biblical message is good news because the Lord loves justice (Isaiah 61:8); is a stronghold to the poor and needy (Isaiah 25:4; Psalm 9:9); hears the desire of the meek, strengthens their hearts, and does justice to the orphan and the oppressed (Psalm 10:17-18); hears the groans of the prisoners and sets free those who are doomed to die (Psalm 102:20); hears the cry of the hungry (Psalm 107:4-6); raises the poor from the dust and lifts the needy from the ash heap (Psalm 113:7); and the Lord maintains the cause of the afflicted and executes justice for the needy (Psalm 140:12). [7]

Our justice system unfairly victimizes the poor who are always over-represented in our prisons, but the priorities of the Old Testament were different. Those laws put less emphasis on theft than other Near Eastern law codes. [8] Theft laws protect the wealthy and are often violated by the needy. Israel's was the only law system where no property crime was a capital offense. [9] "The concern for economic and social equality is further reflected in Israel's special care for people rather than property, for those who did not benefit from her economic system." [10] In contrast, as the following story shows, our justice system shows little concern for economic injustice.

For Some, Crime Pays Well

A decade ago, I was a volunteer in a Victim Offender Reconciliation Program (VORP). This program seeks to bring together victims and offenders, with the hope of achieving restitution and reconciliation with mediation. After working on some minor cases, I was given a daunting assignment: one of the largest cases this VORP had ever tackled. In fact, this case helped VORP receive national media attention. But the most intriguing aspect of the case never made the news.

A dozen youths committed ten break-ins stealing about $70,000 worth of goods. Two youths were involved in all of the break-ins and the other youths each committed only a few break-ins. Plotting the involvements and figuring out restitution obligations was an exercise in frustration. Yet restitution and reconciliation proceeded smoothly.

However, as victims and offenders became acquainted, a

new fact came to light. The youths had taken their stolen goods—jewelry, silver, coins—to two local jewelry stores. The stores were prominent in the community and had a good reputation, yet they had no qualms when these fifteen- and sixteen-year-olds regularly came in and sold valuable goods. In fact, one store made a special arrangement, instructing the boys when to come and whom to deal with. Of course, the stores only paid a small fraction of the actual value of the goods.

When a victim learned this and went to one of these stores she was offered the chance to buy back some of her property. The dealer said that the goods were already in Chicago but might be recovered for a price. Unbeknownst to the store-keeper, the victim was wearing a tape recorder and the police monitored this conversation. In spite of the incriminating evidence, the police filed no charges against the stores.

While the boys had some ill-gotten pocket money, the jewelers took in much more. Not only did they pay small prices for valuable merchandise, they bought it under questionable circumstances. By their complicity in—and exploitation of—the original crime, they furthered the victimization of the victims and contributed to the victimization of the youths. Most of the property was quickly sold and is beyond recovery. Since much of it was of sentimental value, nothing could replace its loss.

The court required the youths to serve jail time and make restitution for their crimes. Although they saved most of the money they received from selling the stolen goods, full restitution was difficult because the youths received such a small fraction of the value of the goods. They would have to work for many years to repay their victims.

The central youth in the break-ins, Dave, was sentenced to probation and eight months of jail time on weekends. An exceptional fellow, he was very cooperative in the restitution and reconciliation process. His meetings with victims all went well. Even skeptical, bitter, and fearful victims were glad to work with him. At the court's order, he sold all his personal possessions, lost his driver's license, went through the "Scared Straight" program and worked part-time for years to pay off his debts. He also worked hard in school. He was paying the full price for his crimes, even though others had made bigger profits from those crimes.

Meanwhile, the police chose not to prosecute the stores in spite of the "sting" operation where a jeweler admitted possessing stolen property and offered to sell it back to victims. I tried to bring this issue to the "court of public opinion" by taking the information to the local newspaper. Reporters interviewed victims, offenders, police, and the local store owners and developed an impressive series of articles. But, for reasons unknown to me, at the last minute, the paper decided not to publish the findings.

In this process, victims lost their sense of security and their belongings. The young offenders lost their reputations and their free time. The jewelers, however, made a profit and evaded prosecution and public scandal.

Retaliation or Restoration?

It is ironic that with the increasing involvement of certain evangelicals in politics there has often come a "law and order" agenda that calls for "getting tough" on crime.

> Protestants are biased against law because we are supposed to be saved by grace, not by works of law. Paradoxically, however, the very people who religiously disparage law are usually the ones most uncritically vocal about law and order. They tend to equate observance of the law of the land with Christian rectitude even while they deprecate "legalism" in religion. [11]

Since Jesus' teaching, example, and work accomplished restoration and reconciliation rather than retribution and condemnation, this has implications for how we view law. Paul gave the law an important place but one that is secondary to *love*: "Love does no wrong to a neighbor; therefore love is *the fulfilling of the law*" (Romans 13:10, emphasis mine). The intent of law is to point to God's priorities: "But now the righteousness of God has been manifested *apart from law*, although the law and the prophets bear witness to it" (Romans 3:21, RSV, emphasis mine).

When Hosea redeemed his adulterous wife, when Joseph refused to shame his pregnant fiance Mary, and when Jesus did not condemn the woman caught in adultery, they were not breaking the law but fulfilling it. "The characteristic purpose of Israelite law is to redeem, not to punish." [12] The law has far-reaching goals. "Furthermore, the purpose of law was to redeem more than the individual. Its purpose was social redemption, *to redeem the entire society*." [13] Such redemption aims for both harmonious "internal economic relations" and a "peaceful world order ruled by the law of Yahweh." [14]

The Bible is deeply suspicious of the world's law and justice. Paul complains: "How dare one of your members take up a complaint against another in the law courts of the *unjust* . . .?" (1 Corinthians 6:1, JB, emphasis mine). Secular courts are unjust because the gospel is not the basis for their understanding of justice. According to God's priorities, his laws are intended to promote peace and the possibility of reconciliation.

For this reason, many Christians conclude that we cannot have anything to do with a system that merely punishes. "Punishment seen as retaliation, whether retaliation by the individual or by society is rejected, *for it alone is the reserve of God. Likewise the state is not allowed to exercise retaliation*." [15] The gospel is the opposite of retribution and thus cannot be used to support retribution. While the gospel gives free pardon to all of us offenders, retribution says: "You can be restored to society, justified, only by expiating your offense under law." [16] Another author is just as forceful: "When we rely on the so-called 'criminal justice system' . . . we are at the same time declaring that the Gospel is irrelevant." [17]

Such authors pose a challenging choice: abide by God's gospel or rely on the state for law.

The Need for Restoration and Reconciliation

The thrust of the Bible pushes us towards justice and law that redeems, restores, and reconciles. Crime is primarily a violation of human relationships.

> Crime affects our sense of trust, resulting in feelings of suspicion, of estrangement, sometimes of racism. Frequently it creates walls between friends, loved ones, relatives, and neighbors. Crime affects our relationships with those around us. [18]

A good friend of mine was subjected to a terrifying crime. For a long while, she found it difficult to trust anyone. Her experience of crime fractured her relationships with those who most cared for her. We often felt that she resented us who had not undergone the same experience. Within a year, she left her good job and her marriage was in crisis.

Crime also violates relationships between victims and offenders. Most crimes are committed between acquaintances. "Even if [victim and offender] had no previous relationship, the crime creates a relationship. And that relationship usually turns hostile. Left unresolved, the hostile relationship in turn affects the well-being of victim and offender." [19] Finally, the crime affects wider society.

The solution is not merely to punish offenders. The response to crime must begin where the problem began, within relationships. "Crime is not first an offense against the state. Crime is first an offense against people, and it is here that we should start." [20] Crime causes harm on several levels (victim, interpersonal relationship, offender, and community) but state-justice or retributive justice only focuses on the violation of law.

Understanding crime in this way makes apparent what the response of biblical justice must be.

> If crime is injury, justice will repair injuries and promote healing. Acts of restoration—not further harm—will counterbalance the harm of crime. We cannot guarantee full recovery, of course, but true justice would aim to provide a context in which the process can begin. [21]

Retribution cannot bring recovery. "In the last decade, the official crime rate has risen only 7.3 percent while the number of people incarcerated has risen by 100 percent; on any given day, 3.5 million men, women, and children are under some type of correctional control—incarceration, probation, or parole; $13 billion [U.S.] a year is spent on federal and state prisons and local jails; per capita spending on prison and jails has increased by 218 percent during the last decade." [22]

Restorative justice works to redress fractured relationships. It works at all levels for victims, offenders, and the commu-

nity. Such justice involves reparation, restitution, and hopefully even reconciliation. This cannot be done easily. It
involves the hard work of confrontation, confession, and forgiveness.

Moving towards the bigger picture of God's justice and the
spirit of God's laws is not easy. It may be easy to feel compassion for victims, but God's bigger picture also calls for compassion for offenders. It may be easy to imprison offenders,
but God calls imprisonment into question and asks us to look
at the true roots of crime. It may be easy to narrowly apply
laws and punish offenders, but God calls us to look at the
bigger picture and to work for a justice that heals and restores
everyone: victim, offender, and community.

For Discussion

1. What purposes does the law serve? Whom does it protect? Whom should it protect? Whom does it afflict? Whom
should it afflict? How do you feel about the present arrangements?

2. What purposes should the law serve? How could the law
be made to serve victims, offenders, and community?

3. Were you surprised by the story of the jewelry stores?
Were the jewelers also offenders? If not, why not? If so, what
would be an appropriate response to their offenses? Do you
think this incident was exceptional or an example of something that often happens?

4. In what ways does the Bible's understanding of law dif-
fer from ours? Are you comfortable with the idea of law as a
flexible teaching that needs application?

5. How does our society put emphasis on retributive justice? Why does it put so little emphasis on distributive justice?
How did this chapter's case studies fit into issues of distributive justice?

6. Should Christians—especially inheritors of the Protes-
tant Reformation—consider law of secondary importance?

7. While the Bible teaches a certain respect toward the state,
does it also cultivate a certain critical suspicion? If so, in what
ways?

8. If we truly believe in God's grace, would we refuse to

rely on state law?

9. How is crime a violation of relationships? How can our response to crime bring healing to relationships?

10. Are many imprisoned offenders themselves victims of distributive injustice? Why?

11. In "Just the Facts, Ma'am," was the young man foolish to defend himself? Should he have been charged? convicted? Was he a criminal or offender? Why or why not? Why is it insufficient to view crime as a violation of state rules? Do you think this case was exceptional, or an example of something that often happens? What would have been a better outcome?

Aids to Reflection

If one thing is clear in the New Testament it is the central theme of the triumph of grace over law.

While Paul stopped short of a . . . complete disregard for law, he did make it clear that to abide in grace is more radical than to abide by law. And such law as he did emphasize was not law in the sense of the entreaties by the State to make us behave, but an ethic, the fruit of the Spirit, resulting from being "in Christ."

—Will D. Campbell and James Y. Holloway, *Up to Our Steeples in Politics.*

A full reading of the Bible introduces us to some surprising twists in the scenario of how evil is responded to. I would like to put the emphasis on *surprise*. This surprising way of responding to evil is sometimes begged for in psalms and prayers, but it is *always* structurally an essentially unwarranted surprise. What is this surprise? It is grace, forgiveness, a new beginning unencumbered by the debts and trespasses of the past, and the offer of reintegration into a community of solidarity and wholeness to those who do not deserve it. It is, to be sure, a trajectory witnessed to throughout the whole Bible, but for us nowhere as clearly and as decisively as in the event of Jesus' life, death, and resurrection.

—Tom Yoder Neufeld, "Reflections on the Biblical Foundation for Restorative Justice Ministries," unpublished manuscript, presented at "The Future of Prison Ministries: A Restorative Vision," Bethel College, October 1987.

The prize for most unusual crime-and-punishment story goes to the O.K. Corral in Tombstone, Arizona. Tombstone Explorations, Inc., dumped 100,000 gallons of cyanide into the soil (and drew a $25 fine). The following day, trucks hauling the tainted material were zipping along the road splashing school children with mud and making them jump off the road. The air was filled with a strong cyanide smell. Gabe Brett, a 62-year old Tombstone grandmother, decided this had to stop, so she, her husband and three neighbors linked arms and made a human chain to block the trucks. When one of the truckers got angry and started waving his arms at Gabe, she slapped him. Well, this was good for a $1000 fine from local Magistrate Alfred Pickett. The fine was overturned on appeal on the condition that Gabe would shake the trucker's hand. She did, but the judge commented that the look on her face was like she had just been made to swallow something awful.

—"Granny fined $1000, Dumper Fined $25," *The Neighborhood Works,* Chicago: Center for Neighborhood Technology, February 1985.

END NOTES

1 Howard Zehr, *Changing Lenses* (Scottdale: Herald Press, 1990), p. 143.

2 Millard Lind, "Law in the Old Testament," *Monotheism, Power, Justice: Collected Old Testament Essays* (Elkhart, Ind.: Institute of Mennonite Studies, 1990), p. 65.

3 Zehr, *Changing Lenses*, p. 143.

4 Martin Buber's term, quoted by Zehr, *Changing Lenses*, p. 144.

5 Hans Jochen Boecker, *Law and the Administration of Justice in the Old Testament and Ancient East*, trans. Jeremy Moisier (Minneapolis: Augsburg Publishing House, 1980), p. 136.

6 Zehr, *Changing Lenses*, p. 137.

7 Jack A. Nelson, *Hunger for Justice* (Maryknoll: Orbis, 1980), p. 184.

8 Boecker, *Law and the Administration of Justice*, p. 166.

9 *Interpreter's Dictionary of the Bible*, vol. 1 (Nashville: Abingdon, 1962), p. 734.

10 Lind, "Law in the Old Testament," p. 71.

11 Marlin Jeschke, "A Christian Approach to Criminal Justice," in *Brethren Life and Thought*, ed. Wally Landes, vol. XXIX (Winter 1984), Number One, p. 36.

12 Lind, "Law in the Old Testament," p. 70.

13 Emphasis added. Lind, "Law in the Old Testament," p. 70.

14 Lind, "Law in the Old Testament," p. 71.

15 Siegfried Meurer as quoted by Wayne Northey in *Biblical/Theological Works Contributing to Restorative Justice; A Bibliographic Essay* (Mennonite Central Committee U.S. Office of Criminal Justice, August 1989), No. 8, p. 11.

16 Jeschke, "A Christian Approach to Criminal Justice," p. 39.

17 Lee Griffith, "Alternatives to Calling the Police: Some Biblical and Historical Perspectives," Unpublished manuscript presented at The Christian as Victim conference, April 1-3, 1982, p. 1.

18 Zehr, *Changing Lenses*, p. 181.

19 Zehr, *Changing Lenses*, pp. 181-82.

20 Zehr, *Changing Lenses*, p. 182.

21 Zehr, *Changing Lenses*, p. 186.

22 Anthony A. Parker, "Crimes of Punishment," *Sojourners* (June 1990), p. 12.

CHAPTER 6

Am I My Brother's Jailkeeper?
A Critique of Imprisonment

Life Sentence

"Killer Recaptured; Linked to Fascists," the newspaper headline screamed. The mug shot showed a desperately dangerous killer, one John Chaif. His thick beard and disheveled hair showed a lack of concern for personal grooming. His glasses sat crookedly on his face, as if he were not smart enough to put them straight. From behind the lenses, beady eyes threatened the world.

You could easily see that this crazed man must be a criminal, someone you would expect to see on Wanted posters, the kind you never want to meet in an alley. What a relief that the authorities had captured him.

I don't know when the picture of John was taken or what the circumstances were, but I know this: he was not captured on the basis of that photo. It bears no resemblance to him. I ought to know; he has been my friend for over a dozen years.

When I visited John in prison, I found him trim, well-groomed, and neat, with a friendly face, a lively smile, and good-humored sparkling eyes. I searched the news articles in vain for a reflection of the man I know.

Karen was a good friend of mine in university. We often shared tea and heart-to-heart chats. Together we started a weekly prayer meeting. When my sister died, I first called my girlfriend and then Karen. They helped me with my grief.

I also got to know Karen's fiance, John, who lived out of town. Hating showers, I dreaded attending Karen and John's wedding shower. But John's humor transformed a potentially trivial time into one of laughter and joy. Later, my future wife, Lorna, and I enjoyed their wedding, a simple morning affair with no tuxedos and only one attendant each. It matched our intuitions that gaudy, expensive celebrations need not be the norm. Lorna and I modeled our wedding after theirs.

I stayed with John and Karen several times, sharing long and hard with them about our faith. They both responsibly pursued their careers, were active in the local church, and lived upstanding lives. They were compassionate people, always caring for others.

One summer day, an old friend phoned me.

"I've got some bad news."

"What's wrong?" My mind ran riot.

"Karen's dead, Arthur."

This was too terrible and unreal. She was only twenty-five.

"Karen's family is having a hard time because John's in jail."

I dumbfoundedly repeated: "John? John in jail?" It did not compute: Karen dead by accident, mishap or disease and her husband in jail?

The story got worse. Karen was shot in the head by a rifle that John was holding. John claimed it was an accident. Karen's parents, close to both John and Karen, believed John's account. In his grief and rage, John was uncooperative with the police and thus was suspected of murder. Her parents later testified to his character before the Supreme Court of Ontario and even paid his bond. Because of their testimony he was subsequently released pending trial; during this time he often visited them.

In 1983, a jury convicted John of first-degree murder and sentenced him to life imprisonment. The judge said the jury made a mistake but felt he had to uphold its decision. Both John's and Karen's families were horrified by this aberration of justice. John did not belong in prison.

He wrote me: "We have a healthy eight per cent of our present prison population being innocent of the crimes they were convicted of committing. This means of the twelve thousand convicts presently in the federal system, one thousand should not be in jail. I am in good company." [1] If Canada still had the death penalty, our friend John would have been a prime candidate.

John's prison accounts were overwhelming and harrowing: smoke, incessant noise, strip searches, lockdowns, petty aggravations, and brutal violence between inmates. I hurt for him and hoped that his spirit could rise above it all. He tried to make the best of it. He took university correspondence courses and considered taking seminary courses, but prison noise made concentration almost impossible. He wrote poetry, tried watercolors, and hooked a rug. His letters arrived illustrated with creative doodles. When I moved to Windsor, his hometown, he asked for tapes of my sermons.

Sensitive reflections were rudely interrupted by surreal surroundings. We compared notes about birding. He mentioned swallows, killdeers, chickadees, whippoorwills, and meadowlarks "in the killing ground surrounding the prison (area cleared for gun towers)." In spite of the killing ground, "I enjoy listening to them all sing and watching them go about their lives."

Sometimes I received several letters a month, ranging from a few paragraphs to six pages. Other times, I did not hear from him for six months. Then he would apologize for his silence. He struggled with grief over Karen's death and bitter anger at his cruel lot. He had little to live for, with no career and no hope of getting out of prison until he was well into his fifties.

John endured aggravations and indignities. It was six weeks before he was given a pillow. A broken toilet went unrepaired for a month and then was fixed incorrectly. Periodically, the prison was locked-up: privileges renounced and cells ransacked, prisoners fed in their cells. Once John received breakfast at 10:30, lunch at 11:30, and supper at 6:30.

John studied and practiced nonviolence. "I can only smile at the man who says 'No' when I ask for a shower. He has not defeated me. God's love for me won't be diminished because I went sweaty for an hour or a day. And by not reacting, it confuses them. In a way, it confuses me too."

Outside life grew unreal. Such ordinary activities as choosing what kind of juice to drink or walking straight for a hundred yards were unimaginable. "I have learned the smell of tear gas and can distinguish between the sounds of a shotgun and a high-powered rifle. I have seen inmates shot by guards. I have heard the angry whine of a ricochet. I have heard, late at night, someone crying and repeating a litany of let-me-dies. I have seen the mutilations of loss of self: self-image, self-respect, self-worth, self-dignity, self-hope. Angry slashes of despair from elbow to palm. And these are the lucky ones. Saved so they can spend their life denied. Forced to ask for a shower, for toothpaste, for a monthly phone call, to risk a hundred times a day the chance of denial and to acknowledge your dependence on another's whim."

Survival became John's preoccupation. "I spend most of my time learning the ins and outs of prison life. Trying to stay out of trouble with prisoners and authorities. A fellow I had gotten to know through Chapel group was stabbed yesterday. A quiet person who didn't bother anyone. He came into the prison lottery. Just came up against the wrong person at the wrong time. We get our ticket with our number. Everybody is a winner."

John asked what Christ would do in such situations. "There have been some prison reforms in the last fifteen years, but not enough. In the two months I have been here two inmates have died at the hands of other inmates. And with a population of less than three hundred I had already come to know their faces. Part of it is the way the prison system strips people of their hope."

John ached for the guilty: "In these acts of violence we all lose. The pain of innocent suffering is nothing compared to the anguish of the guilty. The innocent will heal; the wounded guilty are an open sore constantly picked at." He invited my prayers on their behalf.

We shared reflections about prayer. He responded to my articles and sermons and passed them on to other prisoners. I was ever moved by his compassionate concern. He prayed for me daily and asked probing questions about my life, family, and work. He offered loving counsel and consoled me in my own losses and difficulties.

John struggled mightily against despair. One Easter he wrote. "I have to hold my head up on this block. And that's block as in chopping. They are just going to keep slicing and dicing till there's nothing left of that dream either of us had for our world." Once he wrote: "Just trying to live here takes great quantities of energy, Arthur. For the time being I am well and not without joy, a sure sign that the Holy Spirit is nearby." He had only one true hope. "There are no bars that can keep me from my Lord. The prison is temporal. The fences rust and the concrete crumbles, but God's love has never waned."

For a few months, we exchanged no letters, passing greetings through friends. Apparently he was especially despairing, for John escaped from prison with a convicted bank robber. Suffering another death in order to be "free," he cut himself off completely from family and friends. I prayed for him often, wondering what to make of this deeper silence between us. Many hoped that he could quietly disappear and make a new life for himself.

After thirteen months, he was apprehended. The local press went wild with allegations and lurid headlines. It claimed that John was linked to neo-Nazis, a charge that was later quietly dropped, and that he had participated in a string of continent-wide bank robberies. His continued contention that he did not murder Karen was snidely reported. The ugly mug shots were unrecognizable. Friends said, "That guy looks like a criminal." Mug shots invariably do. When I showed my own picture of John to friends, they saw no resemblance.

What John's Experience Taught Us

This story may not be a usual one, since I and many others contend that John was originally innocent. But John's experience opened our eyes to the horrors of our criminal justice system. It was not just the tragedy of an innocent man being convicted. It was the senselessness of imprisonment. I and many of my acquaintances visited John in prison and were appalled by what we saw. We realized that imprisonment only makes things worse for many offenders, regardless of their guilt or innocence.

If John is now a criminal, then prison made him one. The news alleges expertise in car theft, armed robbery, drugs, guns, and underworld survival. If this is so, he learned this second career in prison. If he committed these crimes, it is partly because his life sentence convinced him that he had nothing to lose. Before being arrested for Karen's death, he had no criminal record.

I protested the media distortions by writing in the local newspaper. For this, some Christians criticized me. Convicts are our contemporary lepers: locked away, separated, cut off. Caring for a convict seems inconceivable to many "decent" people.

Before we heap abuse on a man who may have gone astray, we might ask how our society drove him there. We might wonder why a normal law-abiding person ends up living as a hunted criminal.

Once John wrote about the books and magazines I mailed him: were they risky loans or outright gifts? "It is harder to get things out of prison than to get them in. So anything sent in, if it survives the smash-ups, the fires, the tear gas, water from fire hoses, et cetera, is pretty well lost to the outside world." The fate of gifts symbolizes that of prisoners. It is harder to get people out of prison than it is to get them in.

If they do get out, it is hard to get prison out of them. John wrote: "In a way I have died, because I have tried to deal with life imprisoned. Even if I walk out of here tomorrow, I will never see life the same way." This tragedy scarred many people and may never have a happy ending.

This story raises serious questions about the "criminal justice" practiced in North America, questions that test basic assumptions of our society:

Can innocent people really be sent to life imprisonment or death row?

Besides Karen, who were the victims? Karen's family? John?

What did prison accomplish for John? What do we expect to achieve by tearing a person from normal human society, isolating him in a destructive community, and stripping him of all hope?

The tragedy of John and Karen changed me in ways deeper than intellectual research ever could.

Through my friendship with Karen's family, I came to understand something of the violation that victims endure.

Through my friendship with John and his family, I saw the anger and alienation that prison brings. I realize that the system can wrongly convict. Most importantly, I saw that an inhuman criminal justice system cannot be sensitive to individuals.

The Failure of Prisons

The first American penitentiary was established by Quakers in Philadelphia in 1790. It was intended to be a place of solitary confinement and silent reflection that would lead to repentance or penitence, thus the name "penitentiary." Over the past two centuries, however, rather than achieving this noble goal, prison has instead compounded the problems it was designed to correct.

For example, prison reinforces an offender's tendency to use undue force and coercion. In prison an offender "will learn that conflict is normal, that violence is the great problem solver, that one must be violent in order to survive, that one responds to frustration with violence. That is, after all, normal in the distorted world of prison."[2]

Low self-esteem contributes to criminal activities, yet the entire prison experience is structured to dehumanize—numbers replace names, standardized clothing replaces street clothes, and prisoners have little or no personal space.

> They are denied almost all possibilities for personal decision and power. Indeed, the focus . . . is on obedience, on learning to take orders. In that situation, a person has few choices. He or she can learn to obey, to be submissive. This is the response the prison system encourages . . . . Prison will further deprive an offender of [the] ability [to be self-governing and self-controlled]. Thus it should not be surprising that those who conform to prison rules best are not those who make the most successful transition into the community after prison. [3]

Prison handicaps a person's capacity for healthy human relationships. Because of patterns learned in prison, "domination over others will be the goal, whether over a marriage partner, a friend, or a business acquaintance. Caring will be seen as a weakness."[4]

As we saw in Fred Palmer's case, prison greatly strains families. "Many prisoner families break up during the . . . incarceration. Thus, a prison term often deprives an offender of the basic family relationship which experts agree is absolutely critical to rehabilitation." [5]

The results of such dehumanizing treatment should come as no surprise.

> Instead of rehabilitating offenders, prisons make them worse. The Rand Corporation, in its report *Prisons versus Probation in California*, found that recidivism—repeat offender rates—are actually more serious for prisoners than for identical offenders who were simply put on probation.[6]

The longer a person is in prison, the more pronounced this effect is, and the more likely that the person will use violence in committing further crimes.[7] This is true even though society spends $15,000 to $25,000 per inmate per year on their so-called rehabilitation. Judge Dennis Challeen observes: "We could put a criminal through Harvard for much less."[8]

The Offender as Victim

But if offenders become victims of serious injustice in prison, for most it is hardly the first time. Often injustice contributes to the making of criminals. Offenders certainly bear responsibility for their actions, but the roots of crime often go deep. "Much crime grows out of injury. Many offenders have experienced abuse as children. Many lack the skills and training that make meaningful jobs and lives possible." [9]

Thus the poor are over-represented in prison. Many are awaiting trial in prison simply because they cannot afford to pay the bail to buy their way out of jail.

People of color make up a disproportionate share of prison populations. In the United States, "23 per cent—one in four—of black men ages 20-29 are either in prison, in jail, on probation, or on parole . . . . For Hispanics, the rate is 10.4 percent; and for white men, 6.2 percent. Sixty percent of all females incarcerated are women of color." [10] In Canada, this is reflected by the number of natives in prison. In Manitoba 75 percent of the women in the provincial jail are native Canadians.

Not only are prisons cruel, but they are ineffective. Rather than solving the problems of victimization, crime, racism, they make these problems worse.

What can be done? Can penitentiaries be humanized, made to fulfill their original purpose? Or are prisons so inherently cruel and ineffective that more radical solutions are needed? We'll explore these questions in the next chapter.

For Discussion

1. Do you think that John Chaif's story was unusual or exceptional? In what ways?

2. Discuss the questions on page 71, regarding the case of John Chaif.

3. How does imprisonment reflect retributive justice? How does it contradict the priorities of restorative justice?

4. Were you surprised that Quakers helped start penitentiaries? Where did prisons go wrong?

5. How do prisons compound the very problems they seek to address?

Aids to Reflection

In North America the term "correctional institutions" is still in use, but we know that they do not correct. We have known that since 1960. It has been clear to all scienientific workers in the field. They do not correct. So why do people call them correctional institutions?

—Nils Christie, *Crime, Pain, and Death*, New Perspectives on Crime and Justice: Occasional Papers: Issue No. 1, MCC Office of Criminal Justice, 1984.

Jessica Mitford, in discussing what is a crime, notes that we can find "manufacturers of unsafe cars which in the next year will have caused thousands to perish in flaming highway wrecks, absentee landlords who charge extortionist rents for rat-infested slum apartments, Madison Avenue copywriters whose job it is to manipulate the gullible into buying shoddy merchandise, doctors getting rich off Medicare who process their elderly patients like so many cattle being driven to the slaughterhouse, manufacturers of napalm and other genocidal weap-

ons—all operating on the safe side of the law, since none of these activities is in violation of any criminal statute."
—Jessica Mitford, *Kind and Unusual Punishment.*

Prisons and jails have become a dumping ground for the aged, insane, infirm, poor, and people of color. Nonetheless, prisons and jails remain a fact of life. By incarcerating people—particularly the most vulnerable in our society—without regard to what influenced their crime, we give up hope for them. Unfortunately, it is the financial implications of increased incarceration, and not a moral imperative, that is spurring such a flurry of activity in recent years around prison reform.
—Anthony A Parker, "Crimes of Punishment," *Sojourners,* June 90,

One of four black men in their 20s [in the United States] is either in jail, in prison, on probation or on parole . . . . Violence is the No. 1 cause of death for black males between the ages of 15 and 25; their murder rate is 10 times that of their white counterparts. In California, black males are three times more likely to be murdered than to be admitted to the University of California . . . . Black men in poor inner-city neighborhoods are less likely to live to the age of 65 than men in Bangladesh, one of the world's poorest nations. Black males are the only group that can expect to live shorter lives in 1990 than they did in 1980.
—Ron Harris, *Los Angeles Tribune,* "Life Bleak for U.S. Black Males," *Windsor Star,* July 10 1990.

Because prisoners earn nothing or nearly nothing for their labor, many of them are crushed by the impossibility of helping to support their own families or making reparations to their victims. At the same time, prisons on state and federal levels have become multi-million-dollar industries. An increasing number of individuals and institutions are now economically dependent on prisons' continued existence.
—Murphy Davis, "Prison Slavery," *The Other Side,* May-June 1990.

END NOTES

1 Canadians are still dealing with the fact that Donald Marshall, a Micmac Indian in Nova Scotia, was wrongly convicted of murder and imprisoned for eleven years.

Similar examples can also be found in the United States. The 1988 documentary *The Thin Blue Line* explores the wrongful murder conviction of an innocent man in Texas.

2 Howard Zehr, *Changing Lenses* (Scottdale: Herald Press, 1990), p. 35.

3 Zehr, *Changing Lenses*, p. 37.

4 Zehr, *Changing Lenses*, pp. 38-39.

5 Prison Fellowship, "Liberty to the Captives," *Jubilee* p. 26.

6 Daniel W. Van Ness, David R. Carlson, Jr., Thomas Crawford, Karen Strong, *Restorative Justice*, (Washington, D.C.: Justice Fellowship, 1989), p. 9.

7 Edgar Epp, "Why Prisons Fail," *Catalyst* (March 1982), pp. 13-16.

8 Dennis A. Challeen, "Turning Society's Losers Into Winners," *The Judge's Journal*, p. 7.

9 Zehr, *Changing Lenses*, p. 182.

10 Anthony A. Parker, "Crimes of Punishment," *Sojourners* (June 1990), p. 13.

CHAPTER 7

Can Prisons Be Made to Work?
Humanizing Imprisonment, Creating Alternatives

What Can Be Done About Prisons?

What can be done about the scandal of prisons? Some advocate doing away with all prisons. Others do not go so far, saying that the "dangerous few" need to be incarcerated.

At the very least we should imprison far fewer people. Rates of imprisonment in the United States are higher than in any other industrialized country, including the [former] Soviet Union and South Africa. Many wardens believe that 50 to 90 percent of all prisoners could be released without any threat to the public. [1] And there are many ways to make imprisonment less dehumanizing. Prison Fellowship cites the following options: [2]

1. *Shorter sentences*: "With the possible exception of political prisoners in countries ruled by totalitarian governments, American prisoners serve the longest sentences in the world. In fact, the average sentence imposed on federal offenders in the United States increased steadily from 16.5 months in 1945 to 45.5 months by 1975."

2. *Weekend sentences*: "In cases where long-term continuous imprisonment would wreck an offender's employment or family, the presiding judge may impose a sentence to be served on weekends or other times not disruptive of an offender's responsibilities. We believe, however, that this alternative is much inferior to the use of community service assignments."

3. *Classification*: "As many as 80 percent of American prisoners are incarcerated for nonviolent crimes. Yet placing non-

violent offenders in a penitentiary can often be
counterproductive. Frequently they are subjected to rape,
brutal treatment, the continual threat of violence, and a boring
routine that deadens the human spirit. Studies have shown
that a great many nonviolent offenders come out of prison not
rehabilitated but in far worse mental, physical, and moral condition than when they went in.

"In no case should nonviolent offenders (or those with
demonstrated good behavior records) be housed . . . with
those guilty of violent crimes or behavior. The need for classification in this regard goes far beyond existing designations of
'minimum' 'medium' and 'maximum' security sections within
penal institutions."

4. *Protection against violence*: "Offenders who must be
incarcerated should also be protected against the physical,
psychological, and sexual intimidation which has always been
too much a part of prison life.

"Men and women do not forfeit their right to life and personal safety when they are sentenced to prison."

5. *"Good-time" credit*: "Inmates should have the incentive
of a reduced sentence based on constructive, positive response to their imprisonment. Consistent guidelines delineat-
ing that behavior should replace a system too often based on
caprice or individual bias."

6. *The use of smaller prison units*: "Most studies show that
big penitentiaries breed violence and gang control. And they
suffer as well from poor staff supervision . . . .

"[Smaller prisons] should be located near major population
centers rather than out in the country. This gives both the
family of the inmate and volunteers better access. Generally,
such facilities are also far more humane and manageable."

7. *End mandatory sentences*: Mandatory sentencing was
Fred Palmer's problem (see Chapter 4). They deprive the judge
of "the authority to allow for mitigating circumstances or first-
time offenders."

8. *End "habitual criminal" acts*: Habitual Criminal Laws
call for automatic, mandatory life sentences for people with a
specified number of convictions. "Most prison guards would
favor repeal of mandatory 'habitual criminal' sentences be-

cause such laws make their jobs more dangerous. For instance, a guard in the State of Washington was killed a year ago when he apprehended a two-time offender. The offender 'chose' to kill the guard in the hope of avoiding capture and a third offense that would mean an automatic life sentence. He had nothing to lose and, had he gotten away with it, everything to gain.

"Inmates sentenced under 'habitual criminal' acts are well-known to be the most difficult offenders to manage in a prison. You have little or no incentive to good behavior when you are faced with no hope of release from prison."

Edgar Epp, a Christian, was a warden in a prison where some creative reforms were implemented, including having staff serve without guns. Epp describes the result:

The removal of guns and weapons from all prison staff results almost immediately in a reduction of violence among prisoners, including property damage. When one establishes an atmosphere that says very clearly, "I have no intention of using violence against you," the response is one of less tension, less fear and less defensiveness. Furthermore, staff are thus required to develop their ability in using personal persuasion and human relationship to achieve desired responses, rather than coercion and force. Violence and threats of violence do nothing more than evoke a preparedness to respond with violence or even, in the current language of militarism, to strike first. [3]

Epp observed that many escapes from prison were due to fear of other inmates. He considered it the height of injustice to respond to an inmate's desperate need to escape, possibly even to save his or her own life, by using force. When Epp therefore chose not to prosecute all escapes, the results were surprising. Escapes and escape attempts decreased, many escapees surrendered voluntarily, and most escapees did not arm themselves.

The Limits of Reform

While such measures made imprisonment less dehumanizing, in the end Epp decided that no amount of prison reform could redeem imprisonment. Retributive approaches simply don't bring about restorative results. In an article titled "Why Prisons Fail," he explained why he had concluded that prisons could not be made to work, and therefore should be abolished. [4]

1. "Penal institutions provide the very basis for oppression and the abuse of power. Prisons divide people into two distinct groups, those with power and those without. And power does corrupt . . . . I have seen a 'corrections officer' make his supervisory job easier by reminding the inmates, with a smile, that the officer's opinion of them would be noted by the Parole Board, thus implying that the inmates had better do his bidding without complaint."

2. "Institutionalized people, whether staff or inmates, resist change . . . . When my staff and I began to institute changes in one Canadian prison, such as not using the dark isolation (punishment) cells and by involving prisoners directly in decision-making with respect to their behavior and their future careers, the response was a prison riot. The prisoners were afraid of changes . . . . Most staff were more comfortable with the riot than they were with the changes being made."

3. "Ultimate decision-making in a bureaucracy is political. Perceived expedience and protection of one's image, rather than consideration for what is just, right or merciful, determines most courses of action . . . . A small number of inmates in one of Canada's oldest and most ignominious prisons had set fire to the tailor shop in which were made the drab inmate uniforms for all institutions in that province. The prison in which I was warden at the time was dependent on this shop for its inmate clothing issues. Senior officials decided to introduce disciplinary measures by refusing to issue new clothing until the tailor shop could be restored. A delay in rebuilding resulted in inmates having to wear very worn and tattered clothing. The young men in my prison rebelled. It was not until the politicians and senior officials became worried that a riot based on inmate demands for decent clothing would create bad publicity that arrangements were made for new clothing issues. The question of countless inmates who had nothing to do with the fire being held responsible and being caused the indignity of wearing rags was hardly considered. The fire incident had provided a good excuse to reduce expenditures at inmate expense. Inmate welfare was not the

determining factor in the decision-making of the bureau-crats."

During federal election years, prisoners are often greatly restricted in the hope that there will be no political embarrass-ments such as riots or escapes.

4. "Despite all the apparent failures of prisons to reform criminals or to have any appreciable effect on the crime rate, 'prison reform' is still viewed generally as requiring changes within the prisons themselves rather than developing alterna-tive ways of handling the crime problem . . . .

"New and modern facilities have been developed . . ., com-plete with electronic controls and surveillance mechanisms. New and more sophisticated staff training courses have been introduced. Academic upgrading and trades training courses have been devised for inmates. Counseling and prisoner after-care programs have been offered. And all to no apparent avail, because the dynamics of prisons are such that long-term reha-bilitation and reform are effectively offset by the prisoner's immediate and overriding need to survive the system.

"It is this simple. In order to survive, literally, a prisoner must guard against being cast under suspicion as a possible 'informer' . . . . Even spending too much time in the chap-lain's office can throw suspicion on an inmate. What are they talking about? What is being confessed? How has the adminis-tration found out about hidden weapons, drug 'drops,' illicit alcohol, 'kite' lines (uncensored mail), etc.? Suspected inmates are quickly brought into line or effectively eliminated . . . .

"There is no . . . way of breaking through this syndrome. A caring staff person hardly dares to show love and concern, if for no other reason than the fact that he/she may be throwing suspicion on the inmate to whom concern is expressed!"

5. "Our society . . . is still convinced that force, including violence, is necessary for managing conflict. Our society ap-pears not to be so much concerned about the use of violence but rather with the question of whether or not the violence being used is illegal. We do not tolerate violence used by the 'bad guys,' but we applaud it when the 'good' enforcer, who represents our values, catches the criminal by whatever means."

Epp concludes:
"We blind ourselves to the utter failure and oppressive discrimination of our prison system . . . . We move far too slowly in demanding that corrections authorities and legislators implement such proven alternatives as diversion centers and victim-offender reconciliation programs. We are too reluctant to give of ourselves as friends and sponsors of prisoners . . . .

"In short, we as Christians who embrace a theology of nonviolence have failed to apply the message of love and reconciliation to dealing with those among us who transgress our criminal laws. The challenge to become Christ's witnesses, to reach out with love and a message of reconciliation, to proclaim release to the captives, is before us. The biblical call to do justice and to love mercy remains for us to be answered."

Alternatives to Prison

Reforms can make prisons less dehumanizing, but such improvements are not sufficient for Christians who are called to bring healing and restoration. Rather, we must look for constructive alternatives to imprisonment. Here are some of the available alternatives. [5]

1. *Community service*: "Too often offenders now pay their 'debt to society' in prison. The resulting waste of valuable human resources is easy to document. For instance, the prisoner operating the washing machine next to Charles Colson at Maxwell Federal Prison had been a prominent doctor, convicted of stock fraud. This particular prison had no resident doctor. The many inmates with medical needs had to rely on a paramedic while a qualified doctor spent his days putting dirty underwear into the washing machine. Later, when this doctor volunteered to help meet a shortage of doctors in the surrounding community by working nights, his offer was refused."

Offenders can often make contributions that also enhance their self-esteem. "Some convicted criminals make better volunteers than inmates, says a Windsor provincial court judge." [6] The judge, Saul Nosanchuk, has a 90 percent success rate. In one Indiana county, "during a recent year, over 40,000 hours of free work was provided to sixty community agencies, including governmental and nonprofit organizations. As a form of symbolic restitution to the community whose laws were violated, this program resulted in 8,300 days being diverted from jail incarceration, at an economic value (or benefit) to the county in excess of $300,000." [7]

There are hazards however. "Community service sentencing can become little more than a modern day form of the chain gang." [8]

2. *House arrest*: "This alternative is primarily for convicted felons whose probation reports indicate they are unlikely to be involved in further criminal behavior. Many of those sentenced to house arrest are first-time offenders with no record of prior criminal activity.

"In California, for example, a nurse . . . was sentenced to house arrest for one year for the fatal shooting of her husband . . . . (Mitigating circumstances were present.) The convicted woman was required to report each morning and evening, seven days a week, to the county's probation department. This sentence permitted her to maintain her nursing job and care for her child."

3. *Probation and contract probation*: Probation is a common alternative. "Offenders on probation are sentenced to obey specific behavior guidelines under the supervision of a probation officer. Violation of the guidelines can result in incarceration; so the offender has every incentive to behave." Contract probation often includes community service, restitution, and regular reports to supervisors.

4. *Deferred sentencing*: After conviction, sentencing is postponed for some time while the offender deals with certain agencies (for example, alcohol or drug treatment). The offender's involvement with the specified agency affects the sentence. Positive involvement in drug rehabilitation, for example, might mean probation rather than imprisonment.

5. *Suspended sentencing*: This is what Judge Bontrager attempted in the Fred Palmer case. If an offender abides by certain behavioral guidelines, a sentence remains suspended. If the offender violates the guidelines, then the sentence is imposed.

6. *Fines*: The Prison Fellowship argues that fines could be

used far more widely, especially in cases of nonviolent offenses. However given the fact that so many offenders are
poor, many would not be able to pay. Day-fines, pioneered in
Europe, involve adjustment of fines according to income.
Fines are based on a certain number of days' salary.

7. *Alcohol and drug treatment*: "In June 1978, a special
report to Congress reported that as many as 83 percent of the
people in prison or jail have had some sort of alcohol involvement in their crimes." Alcohol and drug treatment would be
far more productive than prison.

8. *Employment assistance*: Poverty and unemployment are
two major factors in much crime. "Crime may reflect both
personal and societal failure. Yet too often only the convict is
punished. Underlying conditions and attitudes remain un-
changed."

9. *Pretrial intervention*: "Some jurisdictions provide what
is called a 'second chance' system. A first offender or an unin-
tentional lawbreaker is given counseling. After a year, if the
person's conduct is satisfactory, the indictment is expunged
and the record cleared . . . ."

10. *Community dispute and mediation centers*: Community boards with trained mediators can arbitrate cases that
might normally go through the criminal justice system. This
reduces the case load of the courts, keeps disputes within the
community, and deals with offenders within the community.
This is especially helpful with youths, keeping them from
prison and saving them from a criminal record. Victim Offender Reconciliation Programs are an example of this kind of
alternative.

Unfortunately, many alternatives are not used to replace
imprisonment, but as additional means of retribution. Once I
was in court and overheard a judge lecture an offender on why
he was sentenced to community service. It is a "restriction on
your liberties" that is "more productive for the public than
jail." When another offender tried to explain a problem he
was having, the judge cut him off and told him abruptly: "This
is better than dragging a cup back and forth over jail bars."
The courtroom erupted in laughter.

Despite initial intentions, evidence exists that many alternative programs have little impact in reducing prison or jail incarceration because only extremely low-risk offenders are placed in these innovative programs. During the past decade, advocacy and development of alternatives to incarceration and community corrections grew by leaps and bounds throughout the entire country, and yet, the prison population also grew by 60 percent. Strong evidence indicates that an essentially two-track system of punishment is present in American society. Very low-risk offenders who would never have gone to prison in the first place continue to be placed into these new, alternative programs. [9]

There are many ways to deal with criminals without imprisoning them. Yet suspicions linger: are all these alternatives still another way of merely punishing offenders? Do any of them live up to God's restorative and redemptive ideals? We'll continue to explore these questions in the next chapter.

For Discussion

1. In what ways do we rely on force to solve our most serious conflicts? Why? What other means can we Christians rely on? What means can we promote in our society?

2. How do issues of crime and punishment deeply challenge Christians who profess convictions about nonviolence?

3. As Christians, should we oppose prisons even if they did "work" and even if they were economically affordable?

4. How did you feel about the suggestions for making prisons less dehumanizing? Did they go far enough? Is it possible?

5. Given Edgar Epp's critiques of prison, are prison reforms enough or should we find alternative ways of responding to crime?

6. What are some alternatives to prison? Which did you like? Which did you dislike? Which would be most effective? Which seem most in line with gospel values?

Aids to Reflection

It is, in fact, an utterly preposterous process: to put human beings in cages like zoo animals, strip them of their dignity

and decision-making power, allow their families to disinte-
grate, subject them to such violence that most must carry a
knife to survive, force them to live by a code where they never
testify or tell the truth, submerge them in corruption of all
kinds on all sides, force them to live in an atmosphere of bitter
gloom where so many paranoias are nurtured. Then, after
several years of such torment, we shove them out of the front
gate usually with twenty-five dollars, a new suit of clothes and
a bus ticket home, if there is a home anymore. The guard at the
front gate shouts, "I'll see you in two weeks," This is what
society calls "rehabilitation."

To me, it is like throwing a hand grenade into a crowded
movie theater. It is sheer madness.

—Charles Colson, "Towards an understanding of imprisonment and rehabilitation," in *Crime and the Responsible Community*.

Something like an eternity ago, human beings got all caught
up in the illusion that being human is a relatively unimportant
sort of proposition. Here today—gone tomorrow.

What's more tragic, of course, is that in the wake of this
basic error there quickly followed the idea that human beings
are expendable, which easily degenerated into the proposition
that some human beings are expendable. Certain human beings are expendable. Really bad guys are expendable. Guys
with low I.Q.'s are expendable. Anyone who disagrees with
me is expendable. A long time ago, human beings got all
caught up in the illusion that being human is a relatively unimportant sort of proposition.

Well, that's not true. It's wrong. All wrong. And it has always
been wrong. From the creation of the heavens and the earth, it
has been wrong. . . . Our lives have eternal significance. And
no one—absolutely no one—is expendable.

—Martin Bell, *The Way of the Wolf*.

Incarceration is extremely costly to the taxpayer, destroys prisoners' self-esteem, and denies society of prisoners' productiv-
ity. Incarceration also fails to repay victims, is followed by a
high recidivism rate, and ignores accountability for the crimi-

nal wrong-doing.
—Dennis A. Challeen, "Turning Society's Losers Into Winners," *The Judge's Journal.*

Building new prisons as a response to crime reminds me of building new toilets as a response to diarrhea.
—Maryland legislator Wendell Phillips, cited in *The Other Side*, October 1981.

END NOTES

1 Fay Honey Knopp, *Instead of Prisons* (Syracuse: Prison Research Education Action Project, 1976), p. 82.

2 The following suggestions and uncited quotes are from Prison Fellowship's "Liberty to the Captives," *The Other Side* (October 1981), pp. 31-34.

3 Edgar Epp, "Why Prisons Fail," *Catalyst* (March 1982), p. 16.

4 All uncited quotes here are from Epp, "Why Prisons Fail," pp. 13-16. This article specifically compares and contrasts Epp's experience with that of the warden in the movie *Brubaker* that starred Robert Redford.

5 The following list and uncited quotes are also derived from Prison Fellowship's "Liberty to the Captives," *The Other Side* (October 1981), pp. 29ff.

6 Lauren More, "Charity work gives criminals a chance," *The Windsor Star* (Wednesday November 22, 1989), p. 5.

7 Mark Umbreit, *Crime and Reconciliation* (Nashville: Abingdon, 1985), p. 62.

8 Umbreit, *Crime and Reconciliation*, p. 110.

9 Umbreit, *Crime and Reconciliation*, pp. 62-63.

CHAPTER 8

Liberty to the Captives

Restorative Responses to Victims and Offenders

What Then Do Victims Need?

Our criminal justice system does not work well. It does not work well for victims, offenders, or our society. There must be a better way. In this chapter we will look at restorative ways of meeting the needs of both victims and offenders, needs that often overlap.

Justice needs to begin with victims. What do victims need? [1]

1. *Truth-telling*: Victims are often encouraged to be silent by well-meaning family or friends or by self-interested institutions or people afraid of other consequences. Victims need opportunities to express anger, fear, and pain. They need recognition of the right to grieve. "Talking about the pain makes you feel better, not worse,' says Shirley Carr, who lost two sons to homicide in the last year." [2]

2. *Acknowledging the truth*: Victims need to know that they have been heard and that their experience is recognized as significant. "Victims need someone to listen to them. They must have opportunities to tell their story and to vent their feelings, perhaps over and over. They must tell their truth. And they need others to suffer with them, to lament with them the evil that has been done." [3]

3. *Compassion*: While no one can take on a victim's suffering, victims need others to suffer with them. We must overcome the alienating isolation that the pain of crime so often causes.

4. *Protection and help with immediate needs*: Steps must be taken to avoid further abuses and to ensure physical protection: changing door locks, moving away, restraining the offender.

5. *Accountability*: The victim needs the offender to be confronted and held accountable. "Ideally this confrontation results in confession and acknowledgement of responsibility for harm done but frequently this is not the case. But the process of accountability is important regardless of the response of the offender at that point."

6. *Restitution*: "Payment made for damage done is a concrete means of renewing right-relation. Not only is it practically valuable to the victim and survivor but it is highly symbolic." (Imprisonment usually makes restitution impossible.)

7. *Vindication*: Vindication is neither vengeance nor retaliation, but "exoneration for those harmed because the burden of victimization in our cultures is borne by the victim and self-blame is the result. Unlike being a victim of an automobile wreck or being a victim of terminal cancer or a variety of other painful life experiences, when we are being victimized by another person, somehow we are to blame."

A remarkable Australian judge noted during a rape trial that the victim needed vindication and reassurance. After the conviction and sentencing, he consoled her: "You understand that what I have done here demonstrates conclusively *that what happened was not your fault.*" The woman broke down and the judge later learned that this moment had been the turning point where her healing began. [4]

Howard Zehr lists other important needs of victims. [5]

8. *An experience of justice*: "Victims need assurance that what happened to them was wrong, unfair, undeserved. They need to know that steps are being taken to rectify the wrong and to make sure that it does not recur."

9. *Empowerment*: Crime is particularly devastating because it destroys our sense of control over our own lives. "Victims need to have their sense of personal autonomy and power returned to them. Among other things, this means that they need to be informed of and involved in their own case as it

moves through the courts." Thus Justice Fellowship works and lobbies for victims to be actively involved in the criminal justice process.

10. *Answers*: Victims' fears can often be alleviated only when they are allowed to fully vent their questions: "Why did this happen? Will it happen again? What could I have done to prevent it? Victims often rate this need higher than more obvious needs such as restitution."

Mennonite Central Committee has a program called Face-to-Face in St. John's, Newfoundland, and Winnipeg, Manitoba. It brings burglary victims to meet burglars in prison. Victims have a chance to ask pressing questions. (This also helps offenders understand the consequence and impact of their deeds.) There is no attempt to work at reconciliation or restitution, since offenders usually do not meet the victims of their particular crime. Amanda Klippenstein, a frightened burglary victim in Winnipeg, was relieved to have the chance to question and confront offenders; they were surprised by what she shared. [6]

Face-to-Face allows people to get beyond the anonymity of the criminal justice system. The program may work with victims of violent crimes as well. "A recent survey showed that most victims of violent crime are open to meeting an offender; many respondents indicated such a meeting would be an important part of their healing process." [7]

11. *Reassurance*: "Victims need to be assured that it is no sin to be a victim, that what happened to them was wrong and undeserved and is not a reflection on them. They need to know that there is no stigma to being a victim or to being in need. They need reassurance that they are worthwhile individuals and they will not be abandoned by God or their friends."

12. *An experience of forgiveness*: Forgiveness is often difficult but absolutely necessary.

> Victims need to be able to forgive . . . . They need to recognize that revenge is not God's way, that while there must be penalties and consequences for those who offend, seeking suffering for offenders is neither productive nor consistent with God's love. But this cannot be suggested glibly. Real forgiveness is not easy

and cannot simply be willed or forced.

Forgiveness does not mean forgetting what happened; a serious offense cannot, and perhaps should not, be completely forgotten. Nor does forgiveness mean redefining the offense as a non-offense—"It wasn't so bad; it doesn't matter."

Forgiveness is a letting go of the power the offense and the offender have over a person. It means no longer letting that offense and offender dominate. Real forgiveness is in fact an act of empowerment and healing.

But forgiveness may take time. It must come in its own time and cannot be forced. And real forgiveness is possible only through the work of the Spirit. [8]

Retribution or revenge does not bring healing to victims. "Most of us assume that retribution is high on victims' agenda . . . . Victims are often open to non-incarcerative, reparative sentences—more frequently, in fact, than is the public." [9]

Marietta Jaeger is a remarkable woman. Susie, her seven-year old daughter, was kidnapped and brutally murdered. Jaeger worked through the forgiveness for her daughter's killer.

Vengeance, hatred, resentment, grudge-bearing, even deliberate indifference, are death-dealing spirits that will take our lives as surely as Susie's was taken from her. They will destroy us physically, mentally, emotionally, and spiritually . . . . Unforgiveness takes an unbearably heavy toll and ends in death, one way or the other. [10]

Making Offenders Accountable

Programs such as the Victim Offender Reconciliation Program and Face-to-Face show the merits of bringing victims and offenders together. Both offenders and victims need offenders to be made accountable. Offenders need to see the costs and effects of their actions. A man convicted of armed bank robberies casually dismissed his actions as "victimless crimes." He needed to learn an accountability that he did not learn in his trial or imprisonment.

Marietta Jaeger's daughter was kidnapped, brutally assaulted, and cruelly murdered. Marietta and her family went a year with no news of her daughter. She was eventually able to confront and personally forgive David, her daughter's murderer. Later, she began speaking about "the call to forgiveness." She became involved with victim-support work and opposition to the death penalty. She visited prisons throughout Canada and was surprised by the results. She told me:

It has been a phenomenal experience for me. In every case, I was told ahead of time by the person in charge, "Listen, not many guys are going to come. They know the subject matter. For those who do come, they will be in-and-out and up-and-down. They'll get up for a cigarette or out for coffee. They'll be restless and don't take it personally and don't be distracted."

Every time, more men than they could ever have predicted showed up for the presentation. Not only stayed and listened to the whole presentation, but then really participated in the questions and answers afterwards. And a lot of questions about David [the murderer of Jaeger's daughter]. You knew they were asking about themselves. "Can God really love me?" "Can God really forgive me?" And realizing their own need to forgive the people who had so abused them that coming into adulthood they had committed crimes. And coming into consciousness that what they needed as part of their healing process was to be forgiven by the victims. What they want and need more than anything is to receive forgiveness from victims or the victim's family. Yet they are not allowed that by the criminal justice system: they cannot write letters, nothing, they have no contact with victims. Yet that is what they need and desire. Or at least to be able to ask for forgiveness, recognizing they may not be given it.

Not only do victims have an intrinsic need to meet with offenders, but the opposite is also true: offenders need to meet with victims. As you may recall from the opening story in chapter 4, offenders are not permitted to contact victims.

While serving time in prison, [a young offender] had become a Christian. When he was released by the parole board, he reports that they warned him, "We understand that you have become a Christian. That may mean that you want to go back and try to make things right to the victim. If you so much as go near the victim, you will be back here immediately!" An understandable reaction, perhaps, but also a tragedy. [11]

There are instances where it is not suitable for offenders and victims to meet. Zehr notes that

mediation is not always appropriate. The fear may be too great, even with support and assurances of safety. Power imbalances between parties may be too pronounced and impossible to overcome. The victim or the offender may be unwilling. The offense may be too heinous or the suffering too severe. One of the parties may be emotionally unstable. [12]

Yet the present rigid and universal separation of victims and offenders is counterproductive. Encounters can have astounding results. I remember working in VORP with a young man who had broken into a day-care center, destroyed a few doors with a crowbar, and stole a few small things. The director was outraged by the damage. She was skeptical that meeting the offender in the VORP process could have any value, but after some persuasion, she agreed to meet. The victim-offender meeting went well. The offender was repentant and the director recognized his worth. Not only was he permitted to work off the restitution, he was allowed to work *unsupervised* in a building that he had last visited with a crowbar.

The same offender had broken into the house of a middle-aged, single woman. She too was upset and frightened as well as leery of VORP. After several long discussions, she consented to a victim-offender meeting. Janice was so impressed by the offender that she deducted one third of what he owed from the restitution agreement. Dale was grateful. Both expressed hopes of being friends. She extended a standing invitation for him to visit and he gave a permanent offer of help.

Case Study: Victim Offender Reconciliation Group [13]

Inmates at the state prison in Vacaville, California, meet in a group called Victim Offender Reconciliation Group to sensitize themselves to the pain felt by victims and to learn new ways to respond to things that in the past have triggered abusive and sometimes very violent responses.

Richard Early, who works at the prison, brought a few inmates together to be the steering committee for an idea he had heard about related to bringing victims together with offenders. They regularly invite representatives of victims' rights organizations and victims of many different offenses to share how the crime impacted them. Their goal is that the experience will lead toward healing and reconciliation for both victims and themselves.

They named themselves without being aware that anything like VORP even existed. . . . [Eventually, the group met with Ron Claassen and Duane Ruth-Heffelbower of VORP.] They said things like this: "Reconciliation is a spiritual experience, it can't be taken out of that context." "Reconciliation must be voluntary, you can't force it." "When we get out, how can we get involved with VORP?" "Will you have groups we can get involved in for support and to help others not make the mistakes we made?" "I have learned for the first time how my actions affect another. It has changed my relationship with my wife and we can't wait now for me to get out. I used to abuse her." "Every prison needs a group like ours and connections to an outsider group like VORP. How can we work together?" "We have read a little about restorative justice . . ., let's talk about it."

At least six asked if we could help them to meet with their victims when they get out.

Case Study: Teaching Peace in Prison [14]

What do Lovable Les, Victorious Violet, Realistic Roger, and Happy Harold have in common? They were all participants in a Creative Conflict Resolution program held last summer in a prison in New Brunswick.

The program was led by Melodious Mary and Mellow Mark Hurst, Mennonite Central Committee volunteers in Saint John. Ten men and women, chosen by prison officials because of "anger management" problems, participated in the week-long program. Most prisoners had a history of violent behavior.

The positive names were given to participants during an affirmation exercise held the first day. The program concentrated on cooperation, communication, and conflict resolution. We tried to communicate that conflict is a normal part of life and that it can be dealt with in positive nonviolent ways.

The program's effectiveness was tested on the last day when a woman was called out of a session and told that her children were to be taken from her again. The last time this happened she picked up an industrial-size washing machine and threw it. We wondered how she would react this time.

She returned to the session in tears. Within our circle she

had the freedom to cry, spill out her feelings, and tell us how she was dealing with her hurt and anger.

We received many positive comments from the prisoners. "I talk and listen more," said one. "This stuff [conflict] happens all the time. Now I'm slowed down and can see it," said another.

We were pleased. Presenting the program in the prison was a breakthrough for us. Prior to this the prison had turned down our requests for Bible study and visitation programs. So we were pleased and surprised when, after being invited to the prison to explain our conflict resolution program, we were asked: "How soon can you put it on? How about next week?"

We have an opportunity to teach prisoners about the peace Christ brings. We can show that Jesus died not only to reconcile us to God, but to each other.

Restitution Versus Imprisonment

The late Edgar Epp had no hope for our prison system. "I see no effective way of dealing with the failure of prisons other than to abolish them completely and to replace them with community-centered alternatives. Only dangerous offenders are in need of physical restraint and the vast majority of dangerous people are basically emotionally sick people. Their needs would be better met in a hospital setting than in a prison." [15]

Such assertions may seem almost as impossibly idealistic as Jesus' Sermon on the Mount. Much is made of the heinous criminals among us. Television shows broadcast and perpetuate stereotypes of offenders as wicked and clever people attempting the undermining of society. Stereotypes are overcome when victims and offenders encounter one another and the offender grows accountable in the process. "Accountability also involves taking responsibility for the results of one's behavior. Offenders must be allowed and encouraged to help decide what will happen to make things right, then to take steps to repair the damage." [16]

County Court Judge Dennis A. Challeen of Winona, Minnesota, promoted a vigorous program of creative restitution sentencing. [17] He has this assessment of offenders.

With the exception of white-collar and professional criminals who rarely are prosecuted or convicted, the average criminals who appear before most American courts are largely life's losers, misfits, and chemically-dependent unemployables who commit crimes out of impulse rather than plan . . . . Moreover, their negative personalities make them easy targets for hate.

Challeen believes that retribution is based on a myth "that harsher punishment of these losers will curtail crime . . . . The problem is that criminals are not average and do not respond like achievers, who learn from past mistakes."

Challeen enumerates the problems of offenders:

Most are frustrated and angry at themselves and the world; they are very defensive, anti-authoritarian, and feel put down by society. They are irresponsible, quit easily, and are unreliable. They blame others for their problems and avoid responsibility. They consistently lie, cheat, and manipulate to avoid confronting their inadequacies, and they lack a priority system in their lives. They feel little guilt and don't empathize with the people they have hurt. They consistently fail to learn from past mistakes and, because of their low self-esteem, they find it necessary to front with macho, cocky, socially unacceptable behavior and become alienated from normal society. They gravitate toward friends who feel as they do and those friends reinforce their negative feelings about themselves and others. They drift into alcohol and drugs, because the only time they feel decent about themselves or others is when they are under the influence.

Incarceration reinforces those negative qualities.

They become more angry and more frustrated. We further destroy their self-worth. We give them reasons to be more anti-authoritarian, and we take away all their responsibilities. We allow them to blame others, including the courts and the justice system. We lock them in prisons where they lie, cheat, and manipulate each other on a daily basis, and where they come in contact only with equally negative people. We give them no priority system, and we totally alienate them from our communities.

According to Challeen, retribution does not work since offenders generally do not learn from mistakes or punishment. Thus prisons do not work as a deterrent on those with little self-esteem. "If a person doesn't care much about himself, a threat has little meaning."

Challeen believes that restitution sentences can build self-esteem. Restitution, as a response to crime has a long tradition (for example, Numbers 5:5-8; Luke 19:8). "Good sentences . . should require offenders to make efforts toward self-improvement, thus removing them from their roles as losers and helping them to address personal problems and character defects that alienate them from the mainstream of society." Restitution positively affects victims, the community, and the offenders, all of which are, at best, ignored in the present criminal justice system.

Challeen asks offenders what they will do to make right their offense, reserving the right to reject inappropriate or unfair sentences.

> Offenders must be involved in their sentences as responsible adults . . . . Forcing a sentence down their throats only reinforces the defensive resentment . . . and causes further alienation. Involvement gives them dignity. Degrading and negative restitution must be avoided. Making fools of offenders or making them feel like part of a chain gang is counterproductive to creating self-esteem.

This way offenders can take responsibility for their wrongs. "Restitution that destroys self-worth is probably worse than the degradation of incarceration from the standpoint of self-esteem."

Moreover, restitution directly benefits society. "Restitution sentencing saves taxpayers' money, it builds self-esteem, and it makes a productive individual out of the offender." Restitution sentencing resulted in only 2.7 percent repetition rates over five years, as opposed to 27 percent repetition rates for jailed offenders!

Prison Research Education Action Project lists several of restitution's impressive assets:

- It keeps the lawbreaker in the community, permitting him/her to correct the original wrong.
- In some measure, it corrects the discomfort and inconvenience caused the victim.

- It brings the victim and wrongdoer together as human beings, not as stereotypes.
- It lessens the community's need for vengeance and contributes to needed reconciliation and restoration.
- It saves the community, the state, and the affected individuals the economic and psychic costs of trial and probable imprisonment.
- It reduces the role of criminal law. [18]

Even so, we must be careful not to let restitution deteriorate into another form of retribution.

Restoring Offenders

Offenders are the lowest class in society. They are treated in ways far beyond what is permissible for "normal" citizens. We try to ignore prisoners. American prisons, for example, are often found in remote rural areas. Offenders are treated as state property to be used and disposed of as the state sees fit. They experience arrests, interrogations, trials, jails. They lose control, privacy, and sense of dignity.

Maurice McCrackin, a seventy-year old Presbyterian preacher, was kidnapped by two escaped inmates in 1978. He was eventually released unharmed. He was later called before a grand jury to testify against the men. He refused, out of conscience, because he opposes imprisonment. He was cited for contempt and held until he would agree to testify. After four months, the court realized that McCrackin would not change his mind and finally released him.

I have noticed the prevalent stigma against offenders in other instances too. Many of my relatives and friends seem shocked when they learned that I visit an inmate friend.

The fact that society regards offenders as least important is reason enough for Christian involvement. Jesus spent much time being with, affirming the value of, and ministering to those who were rejected in their own society: lepers, tax collectors, prostitutes. Biblical people, knowing that they were once enemies of God and now reconciled to God, know the value of all persons. Biblical people incarnate their faith by involving themselves with those whom society writes off.

Not surprisingly, victims have prejudiced stereotypes of offenders and often they are initially unwilling to meet. One victim needed an hour-and-a-half discussion before she could be persuaded to meet four young burglars. She saw no point, knowing the offenders were worthless. But after meeting the youths, she confessed her respect for them: it took courage for them to meet her. They were brave enough to meet her. She even thanked them for not making a mess during the robbery! The victim moved from feeling sorry for herself to reevaluating the offender.

It is not enough to work with offenders. It is not enough for restitution to be made by offenders to victims. We need to be convinced of the worth of the offenders, ministering as siblings not as paternalistic superiors. The victim needs to affirm the worth of the offender. The offender needs to be convinced of his own worth. This is nothing short of declaring the gospel, God's good news: "the church is under mandate to remind all people of the worth offenders have in the eyes of God and that God loves them even when they do bad things." [19]

For Discussion

1. Do you think that all or most offenders should experience incarceration? Why or why not?

2. Is it realistic to think that alternatives will solve crime? Do prisons solve crime? Can we be content with lessening the damage caused by crime?

3. Why should we be careful that alternatives not be simply retributive?

4. Is there any place for punishment in our criminal justice system? Why or why not? What could punishment accomplish?

5. How can restorative alternatives bring healing? How are victims helped? offenders? the community?

6. Why do offenders need to be made accountable? For their own good? How? For the good of victims? How?

7. What did you think about the Victim Offender Reconciliation Group?

8. What did you think of teaching peace in prison?

9. Does the Christian emphasis on forgiveness disqualify us

from promoting restitution? Why or why not?

10. Do you agree with Edgar Epp that there is no hope at all for our prison system or any prison system?

11. According to Judge Dennis Challeen, what is it about offenders that makes prisons inevitably prone to failure?

12. Is it reasonable to gradually change the criminal justice system from its present retributive extreme of imprisonment to a variety of lesser retributions and eventually to restorative ideals? Or must we completely give up retributive ideas and only embrace ideals of restorative justice?

13. Is it realistic or naive to involve offenders in determining their own sentences?

14. How do you feel about offenders? What stereotypes do you have? How many offenders do you know well? What are you willing to do to break down your stereotypes?

15. Study the offenders in 2 Samuel 11:1—12:23 and John. 7:53—8:11. What were their needs? What had to change? How? Were they punished or restored?

Aids to Reflection

As judges, we are kidding ourselves if we think we are doing society a favor by locking up most property criminals. We are clogging our prisons with them and the evidence clearly indicates that incarcerated criminals get worse rather than better, often progressing to more violent crimes when released.

—Dennis A. Challeen, "Turning Society's Losers Into Winners," *The Judge's Journal.*

Justice is not seen by either Isaiah or Jesus as opposed to love. It is rather the power of God to enable persons again to live in harmony with Him. Since Christians believe Jesus to be the prototype of the human, it may be valuable to look at some concrete instances in which He turned aside the traditional ways of dealing with injustices. It must be noted, however, that for Christian ethics "love must be understood as righteousness in the biblical meaning of that word, as faithfulness regarding God's commandment to preserve this creation, . . . making the world a fit place to live in."

—William Klassen, *Release to Those in Prison.*

Thus the church is under mandate to remind all people of the worth offenders have in the eyes of God and that God loves them even when they do bad things. It does so by ministering in whatever ways it can to those who have violated the laws of society and now find themselves removed from society. It does so also by working for better ways of preventing crimes of all kinds, by seeking better ways of dealing with offenders than our present system employs, and by showing concern for victim as well as for the offender. For when the church embodies the good news that love has conquered hate (it has done that in the person of Jesus Christ), it is saying to the world: Our King has come and he has declared a general amnesty for all. He throws open the prison gates and releases persons from all bonds which confine them. He kindled the light of hope in the eyes of those for whom the world had become too difficult and in doing so led the way for others to follow.

—William Klassen, *Release to Those in Prison.*

END NOTES

1 These first seven points and the uncited quotes here are taken from Marie Marshall Fortune, *Domestic Violence and its Aftermath* (Mennonite Central Committee U.S. Office of Criminal Justice, Occasional Papers No. 9, August 1989), pp. 6ff.

2 *The Mennonite* (January 23, 1990), p. 39.

3 Howard Zehr, *Changing Lenses* (Scottdale: Herald Press,1990), p. 191.

4 Daniel W. Van Ness, et al, *Restorative Justice: Theory* (Washington D.C.: Justice Fellowship, 1989), p. 6.

5 The following points and uncited quotes herein are from Howard Zehr, *Who Is My Neighbor?* (Mennonite Central Committee U.S. Office of Criminal Justice pamphlet), p. 8.

6 Mennonite Central Committee, "Burglary victims and offenders meet face-to-face," *Mennonite Reporter* (16 April 1990), p. 5.

7 John Longhurst, "Face to face: Burglary victims meet offenders," *Mennonite Central Committee Contact* (June 1990), p. 3.

8 Zehr, *Who Is My Neighbor?*, pp. 8-9.

9 Zehr, *Changing Lenses*, p. 193.

10 Marietta Jaeger, *The Lost Child* (Grand Rapids: Zondervan, 1983), pp. 115-16.

11 Zehr, *Changing Lenses*, p. 52.

12 Zehr, *Changing Lenses*, p. 206.

13 This case study was written by Ron Claassen, "VORG," *Criminal Justice Network Newsletter*, Mennonite Central Committee U.S. Office of Criminal Justice, vol. 11 no. 3 (July-August-September 1989), p. 6.

14 This case study is by Mark and Mary Hurst, "Teaching peace in prison: Conflict resolution for inmates," *Mennonite Central Committee Contact* (August 1989), p. 4.

15 Edgar Epp, "Why Prisons Fail," *Catalyst* (March 1982), p. 15.

16 Zehr, *Changing Lenses*, p. 42.

17 All uncited quotes here are from Dennis A. Challeen, "Turning Society's Losers Into Winners," *The Judge's Journal*, pp. 6-8, 48-49. Used by permission.

18 Fay Honey Knopp, *Instead of Prisons*, (Syracuse: Prison Research Education Action Project, 1976), p. 53.

19 William Klassen, *Release to Those in Prison* (Scottdale: Herald Press, 1977), p. 33.

CHAPTER 9

The Restorative Justice Vision
What Can Christians Do?

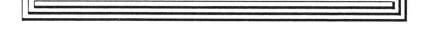

Whose Side Are You On?

Wayne Northey describes an incident that occurred when the Victim Offender Reconciliation Program was beginning in Kitchener, Ontario:

I was program director, working in the same office as Probation and Parole. One of the probation officers contacted me, indicating that he had a probationer who had been charged with three counts of break, enter, and theft. The probationer had admitted guilt to the officer. The officer in turn supplied me with the addresses of the three victims, and the request that I attempt a victim-offender meeting with each of them.

One day the local police phoned, requesting that I go to the police station. Complying, I was ushered into a small interrogation room where two detectives stood. One remained standing at the door and the other instructed me to be seated. Then, rapid-fire, he asked me my name, address, phone number, et cetera. I was taken aback and instantly felt intimidated, realizing that I was being interrogated for an unspecified crime!

It quickly became apparent that these were the detectives working on the cases that had instigated the three break, enter, and theft charges against the probationer. What incensed them, however, was my interference with "due process" by contacting the victims before a plea had officially been entered at court. It mattered not one bit that the probationer had informally admitted guilt to his probation officer and had indicated a willingness to seek to make amends for his wrongdoing. No. They, in fact, wished to charge me with interference with due process.

It took a phone call to the probation officer in question to clear the matter up. At the detectives' insistence, the officer was told by the Crown in no uncertain terms that the criminal process took complete precedence over any thought of amends-making or offering of apology. "Due process" was all-important.

It taught me a valuable lesson. People in the legal system are trained simply to play the game and have an immensely narrow range of vision about what an appropriate response to crime is. Jesus would say: the criminal justice system was made for humanity, not humanity for the criminal justice system!

The Hazards of Involvement

Whenever we involve ourselves in criminal justice issues, we risk many such misunderstandings. Our work with victims may be regarded suspiciously by offenders. Advocacy for offenders may be resented by victims or resisted by the government.

How should Christians be involved? People of faith have responded to this issue with astoundingly diverse approaches.

• Some are involved in prison visitation programs (e.g., M2/W2) and prison Bible studies.

• Some are prison chaplains. [1]

• A Mennonite woman is a member of the Chicago police force and justifies carrying a gun on the basis of Romans 13.

• Edgar Epp, former prison warden, concluded that he had to quit that job. Reflecting on the perfect love of enemies (as recommended in Matthew 5:8-42), he wrote:

> Jesus' words are clearly in harmony with the unfolding Judaic discernment of reconciliation and peacemaking being integral components of justice. As someone trying to integrate these concepts into my lifestyle, I found it increasingly difficult to cope with being a part of the corrections system. I had to conclude that our Canadian criminal law and its concomitant sanctions are not based on justice as I understand the meaning of that word. [2]

• Some are involved in developing alternatives such as VORP, Community Mediation, and restoration programs for convicted murderers.

• An acquaintance asserts that it is a sin even to call the police. He says that calling the police is equal to declaring the gospel of Jesus Christ irrelevant. [3]

• One friend argues that Christians cannot cooperate with the state on criminal justice issues. Griffith echoes such sentiments when he insists:

> Fundamentally what we do is nothing. Even though prisons are demonic manifestations of the fallen principalities and powers, we cannot hope to tear down the walls of the world's prisons, nor is that our task. It is God who frees the captives . . . . While we cannot establish God's Kingdom, we are freed to witness to it. [4]

• Some cope with being victims; others struggle with the reality and consequences of being offenders.

• Some seek to make legislative changes, either as lobbyists or lawmakers. A Canadian cabinet minister, who professes Christianity, favors reinstating the death penalty.

• Earlier, we learned of Maurice McCrackin who refused to testify against the escaped prisoner who kidnapped him.

Several things are clear: we must be involved in such matters, many approaches are needed, and we ought to be humble in our involvement. As Howard Zehr warns: "All this raises many questions, of course, and suggests many dangers. Good intentions can, and often do, go awry; just look, for example, at the history of prisons, which were advocated by Christians with the best of intentions." [5]

Not only are we prone to serious errors in this field, we have clearly seen that the state's retributive means fall far short of the biblical goal of restorative justice. We are called to continued involvement, in spite of setbacks and hazards. While we ourselves cannot hope to achieve God's kingdom, we are called to advance its cause. "It is God's strategy that his law is to rule the world; that is what Jesus and the church are about." [6]

The Media's Message

Not all can get involved with the state on matters of criminal justice. Nevertheless, we are all exposed to the media, which inevitably shapes our understandings and attitudes towards victims, offenders, crime, and punishment. All of us read newspapers, with their tendency to sensationalize crimes. All of us are exposed to movies and television shows and mystery novels, which stereotype offenders. Thus we need to take a critical look at media.

Gerbner & Gross report a direct relationship between the amount of time spent watching television and a "fortress mentality." Heavy viewers of television are more likely to over-estimate the proportion of the general population involved in police work. They are more likely to over-estimate the danger of their own neighbourhood. They are more likely to have a sense of fear about daily life. They are more likely to over-estimate the probability of being involved in a violent crime . . . . While people are aware that events portrayed on television are not "really" happening, they believe that television accurately indicates that such things happen, how they happen, when they happen, where they happen, and to and by what sort of people they happen. [7]

Any daily newspaper or any television news report reveals that the media is obsessed with crime. Why is crime so central to media "news"? "Studies have found that it is so in part because it sells. People are drawn to the sensational." [8]

Another reason crime is prominent in newspapers and television is because it is easy to get information on offenses through local police or the legal system. Moreover, the issues appear clear-cut, with obviously good guys (victims, police, or prosecutors) and readily identifiable bad guys (offenders). No moral grayness here. Unfortunately, reporters generally (and almost exclusively) rely on official sources, in spite of the fact that those sources have a built-in bias.

By superficial reporting on crime, the media gives the appearance of providing social coverage. Unfortunately, this reinforces stereotypes of offenders getting off easy and simply needing a firmer hand and stricter retribution. It further isolates, separates, and alienates offenders from "decent" society.

Al Wengerd has worked in prison ministries for many years. He laments that too many prison ministries are based on the effort to convert inmates. This approach can keep us from facing the fact that we and our society need conversion. The media functions similarly. Very seldom does it raise probing questions about how our society contributes to crime or what responsibility we have to restore victims and offenders.

Politicians are quick to use simplistic portrayals of crime issues to political advantage. A major theme in the 1988 presidential election was a parole program in Massachusetts. The Willie Horton campaign was also not-so-subtly racist, invoking white fears of rampaging black criminals. Zehr argues that the combined effect of media coverage and political exploitation is the mystification and mythologizing of crime in ways that makes us more fearful. [9]

It is easy to focus on offenders as the "scum of the earth." Such self-righteous we-them thinking does not promote restoration. Kit Kuperstock invites her readers to admit to themselves the worst thing they ever did in their lives: income tax cheating, impaired driving, cheating on an important exam, angrily abusing a family member. Then she asks:

> How would you like for a sensitive feature writer for the daily newspaper to do an in-depth piece on that worst thing you ever did, so all the readers will really understand how it was? No? Maybe it would work better to share publicly in church next Sunday? What would the effect on you be if every time your name was mentioned or printed you were identified by that one lowest moment? [10]

For the rest of his life, if my friend John Chaif ever has the misfortune to be in the news again, he will no doubt be succinctly labeled as a "killer."

The focus of crime reporting is usually on violent crime, creating the impression that most crimes are violent. Yet 90 percent of all serious crimes are nonviolent (i.e., usually property crimes).

Moreover, the violent crimes reported are usually a select group. A simple rule applies: the more heinous, the more exposure. We know much about anonymous serial killers. Their names or nicknames are household words: *Son of Sam,*

the Boston Strangler, Richard Speck, the Yorkshire Ripper, Jack the Ripper, Charles Manson, the Zodiac Killer.
While such crimes are exceedingly horrible, they are also exceedingly rare. "If a newspaper features the birth of a two-headed calf, people realize the story is reported because it's a rare occurrence. But when crime is headlined, people become convinced that it's all around us." [11] Most murders (like most kidnaping and most assaults,) occur between people who know one another. "Statistically, we are in more danger of assault, murder, and sexual abuse at home with our families than on presumably crime-ridden city streets." [12]

News coverage of crimes is often racially biased. In Chicago in 1973, a Community Renewal Society study found that 70 percent of murder victims were African-Americans. Only 15 percent of murders were committed by people of a different race than their victim. Phil Blake checked the *Chicago Tribune's* reporting of murders.

> While only 20 percent of the murder victims during this period where white, nearly half of the murder stories were about white victims. Up front in the paper, where readership is high, the imbalance was even stronger—two-thirds of the murder stories on pages one [through] five involved white victims.
>
> To state the statistics another way, a white person slain during this period had a one-in-two chance of being mentioned in the paper, and a one-in-seven chance of winding up on pages one [through] five. But the chances of a Black victim making it into the paper was one in seven, and of winding on pages one [through] five, one in 100.
>
> From this it would seem that the public could draw simple and erroneous conclusions about crime: middle class whites are the most frequent victims of murder. In fact, as the Community Renewal Society survey showed, most violent crime is confined to poor Blacks—poor Black victims attacked by other poor Blacks in their neighborhood. [13]

It is crucial that Christians learn to read between and behind the lines of newspapers. We must also gain skills at doing our own research or finding other reliable sources. Most of all, our hearts and spirits should be informed by biblical compassion and discernment, not by hysteria and misinformation.

Analyzing the Media's Treatment of Crime

Eleanor MacLean has a helpful checklist for monitoring the media, especially newspapers. [14]
• What importance is the item given?
Prominence: On what page is the article found (or at what point in the newscast)?
Space: How many inches of space were used? What was the size of print.
Other significant considerations: How many items of news appear on one story? Were there any news stories neglected? Do you agree with how the newspaper rates the importance of news items in relation to other items?
• Are any *photographs* or *illustrations* used? How are they used? Are they favorable or unfavorable towards their subject? Consider for example the use of mug shots.
How often are pictures used for a certain issue? Are they large or small? color or black-and-white? What do the photographs emphasize?
• Can you identify the important *sources* for the article? Is the source a wire service?
Can you clearly identify who is being quoted in the story (name, occupation, relation to the story)?
• What *angle of the story* is emphasized?
Are humorous comments used? What do they intend? admiration? ridicule?
• What *information* is provided? Are there questions still unanswered? Are they important?
What proportion of this story is straight facts? What is the proportion of opinions (of either the reporter or persons quoted)?
• Was there any prejudicial or emotional use of language that revealed a reporter's *bias* or *point* of view? Were you able to discern a particular attitude towards certain issues or persons?

What Can We Do?

Christians can volunteer with local agencies that address criminal justice issues: halfway houses, community mediation programs, victim-support groups, and prison reform organizations like the John Howard Society and Elizabeth Fry Society. Some of us might also be moved to join or even start restorative alternatives such as the Victim Offender Reconciliation Program in our own communities.

Possibilities are endless. For too long the church has ignored victims and we must certainly not continue that omission. For too long we have also been tempted to scapegoat offenders just as society does. (Remember that working for restorative alternatives for offenders is also in the interest of victims and promises healing for many.)

Consider the following possible activities:

• We can first become informed and aware of courts and prison in our own communities. There are many opportunities to visit with police, lawyers, prosecutors, defense attorneys, victim-support groups, prison officials, and prisoners. It must be recognized that everyone will probably have certain biases. All of the above people can be invited to church. [15]

• Will D. Campbell points out that there are approximately as many congregations in the United States as there are offenders annually released from prison (most of whom will become repeat offenders).

What would happen if each congregation . . . took one of those who is released (just one), offering the same fellowship, support, and hope they extend to all other communicants? Do we doubt that the recidivist rate would be drastically reduced? If we do, then we don't really believe what we say we believe. [16]

• Campbell goes on to take Matthew 25:36, 39, 43 literally when he notes that the number of people in prison roughly equaled the number of churches: "And what would happen if each of the congregations took as their own just one of the . . . men and women remaining in prison, visiting them each week, bringing word from the free world to the prison, returning to the congregation with word from prison, hearing their story, telling them ours? Do we doubt that such a program would result in more prison reform than this nation has ever imagined?" [17] Prisons often offer many volunteer opportunities (e.g., tutoring, vocational training).

• Kuperstock insists on the essential need for us to go and

worship with those in prison as well as welcome prisoners who are released. [18]

• Howard Zehr suggests ways we can support victims: We must openly recognize and acknowledge the intense feelings that crime creates in ourselves and others. We must stand with our sisters and brothers when they are victimized. We can provide assistance to victims. We can help victims grapple with their faith questions. We can help move society to solutions that heal. [19]

For Discussion

1. Select some articles on criminal justice from your local newspaper. Analyze them according to the checklist on page 109.

2. Why were the detectives so threatened by Wayne Northey's restorative efforts in the opening case study?

3. Can Christians work meaningfully on behalf of both victims and offenders?

4. What are some ways that Christians are involved in criminal justice issues? Which forms of involvement do you most admire? Why? With which approaches do you disagree? Why?

5. What are some of the criminal justice issues on which Christians are divided?

6. Describe the role and activities of any of your acquaintances who are involved in criminal justice issues. What have you learned from them?

7. Would you like to see your church more involved in restorative justice? What could it do?

8. What did you learn about the media in this study? Analyze a newspaper, a news program, or a police show to see how it presents crime.

9. How have you been affected by the media in these areas?

10. Given the problems with the media, would it be better to abstain from newspapers or television? Why or why not?

11. How can we encourage the media to be more responsible? Is this a worthwhile endeavor?

12. What will you do to promote restorative justice?

Aids to Reflection

Most of us are not telling the public that there is relatively little the police can do about crime. We are not letting the public in on our era's dirty little secret: that those who commit the crime that worries citizens most—violent street crimes—are for the most part, the products of poverty, unemployment, broken homes, rotten education, drug addiction and alcoholism, and other social and economic ills about which the police can do little, if anything.

Rather than speaking up, most of us stand silent and let politicians get away with law and order rhetoric that reinforces the mistaken notion that police—in ever greater numbers and with more gadgetry—can alone control crime. The politicians, of course, end up perpetuating a system by which the rich get richer, the poor get poorer, and crime continues.

—Robert J. Di Grazia, Boston Police Commissioner, *Parade*, August 22, 1976 as quoted in Fay Honey Knopp, et al, *Instead of Prisons*, Prison Research Education Action Project.

Anxiety about crime is an opportunity. Like most opportunities, it can be seized for good or for ill. It can be used, as it has been, for wind in the sails of those who would glide into power with meaningless promises.

—Gilbert M. Cantor as quoted in Fay Honey Knopp, et al, *Instead of Prisons*, Prison Research Education Action Project.

Actual presence of Christians in prisons has multiple advantages. By definition it improves conditions at the prison, since they are providing needed service, and, since institutions which are routinely visited by the community cannot become snake-pits as easily as institutions which the community ignores. Christian presence is also the most effective means of touching the lives of those in prisons, both prisoners and staff. It makes Christian faith concrete, and gives it credibility. Both staff and inmates will recognize what you stand for if you remain true to your ideals, and this example will have far more impact than anything which occurs outside of prison walls. Finally, actual involvement keeps us from becoming stale in

faith, from preaching but never practicing what we believe.
—Gerald Austin McHugh, *Christian Faith and Criminal Justice: Toward a Christian Response to Crime and Punishment.*

END NOTES

1 Kit Kuperstock reflects helpfully on prison chaplains in chapter 10 of *Worried About Crime?* (Scottdale: Herald Press, 1985), pp. 129-36.

2 Edgar Epp, *Lawbreaking and Peacemaking*, Canadian Quaker pamphlet, no. 15 (Argenta Friends Press, November 1982), p. 10.

3 A brief and particularly insightful analysis on the problem of using police can be found in Jean Lassere's *War and the Gospel*, trans. Oliver Coburn, (Scottdale: Herald Press, 1962), pp. 192-96.

4 Lee Griffith, *Brethren Life and Thought*, ed. Wally Landes, volume XXIX (Winter 1984), Number One, p. 18.

5 Howard Zehr, *Retributive Justice, Restorative Justice* (Mennonite Central Committee U.S. Office of Criminal Justice, Occasional Papers No. 4, September 1985), p. 13.

6 Millard C. Lind, "Law in the Old Testament," in *Monotheism, Power, Justice: Collected Old Testament Essays* (Elkhart, Ind.: Institute of Mennonite Studies, 1990), p. 75.

There are many fine resources on the Christian's relationship to the state:
Vernard Eller, *Christian Anarchy* (Grand Rapids: Eerdmans, 1987). See especially chapter 8.

Wayne Northey, compiler, *Crime Is a Peace Issue* (Mennonite Central Committee Canada Information Services, 1981). See especially Sections II and III.

Daniel W. Van Ness, David R. Carlson, Jr., Thomas Crawford, and Karen Strong, *Restorative Justice* (Washington D.C.: Justice Fellowship, 1989). See especially pages 26-27.

John Howard Yoder, *The Politics of Jesus* (Grand Rapids: Eerdmans, 1972). See especially chapters 8 and 10.

Perry B. Yoder, *Shalom: The Bible's Word for Salvation, Justice, and Peace* (Newton: Faith and Life Press, 1987). See especially chapters 7 and 8.

Howard Zehr, *Changing Lenses* (Scottdale: Herald Press, 1990). See especially chapter 11.

Howard Zehr, *The Christian as Victim* (Mennonite Central Committee U.S. Office of Criminal Justice), pp. 20-21.

7 Ontario Royal Commission vol. 6 (1976), p. 294 as quoted in *Between the Lines: How to Detect Bias and Propaganda in the News and Everyday Life* by Eleanor Maclean (Montreal: Black Rose Books, 1981), p. 17.

8 Zehr, *Changing Lenses*, p. 58.

Kit Kuperstock asks: "Suppose journalists were convinced that front-page coverage was causing more crime? How much restraint would they, and should they, put on covering the news?" *Worried About Crime?* (Scottdale: Herald Press, 1985), p. 75.

Neil Postman has written a devastating critique of the transformation of news into entertainment: *Amusing Ourselves to Death* (New York: Penguin, 1985). See especially chapter 7. "The result of all this is that Americans are the best entertained and quite likely the least well-informed people in the Western world. I say this in the face of the popular conceit that television, as a window to the world, has made Americans exceedingly well informed" (p. 106).

9 Zehr, *Changing Lenses*, pp. 57-59.

10 Kuperstock, *Worried About Crime?*, p. 35.

11 Kuperstock, *Worried About Crime?*, p. 74.

12 Kuperstock, *Worried About Crime?*, p. 35.

Umbreit adds: "We are also more likely to be killed on the road by a drunken driver than by the unknown, unscrupulous, unloving criminal that many of us fear." (*Crime and Reconciliation*, Nashville: Abingdon, 1985, p. 43). In 1990, a man of Mennonite descent was the first Canadian to receive a life sentence because of his history of impaired driving.

13 Phil Blake, "Race Homicide and the News," *The Nation* (December 7, 1974), pp. 592-93, as quoted in Fay Honey Knopp, et all, *Instead of Prisons*, (Syracuse: Prison Research Education Action Project, 1976), p. 160.

14 Maclean, *Between the Lines*, p. 59.

15 Gerald Austin McHugh, *Christian Faith and Criminal Justice: Toward a Christian Response to Crime and Punishment* (New York: Paulist Press, 1978), pp. 206-08.

16 Will D. Campbell's Foreword in *Worried About Crime?*, by Kit Kuperstock, p. 10.

17 Will D. Campbell's Foreword in *Worried About Crime?*, by Kit Kuperstock, pp. 10-11.

18 Kuperstock, *Worried About Crime?*, p. 132.

19 Howard Zehr, *Who Is My Neighbor?* (Mennonite Central Committee U.S. Office of Criminal Justice pamphlet), pp. 10-12.

Epilogue
by Ron Claassen

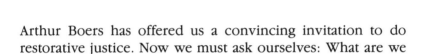

Arthur Boers has offered us a convincing invitation to do restorative justice. Now we must ask ourselves: What are we going to do with it?

I'd suggest we start by committing ourselves to a long-range goal: developing a church-based Victim Offender Reconciliation Program (VORP) in every community.

You have taken the first step by studying this book. If a VORP exists in your community, go with a friend to the next training session. As you work with VORP cases, you'll be amazed at the new insights you will have on the Scripture, "Blessed are the peacemakers."

Why shouldn't the day come when there is a VORP in every community? Why shouldn't our first response to crime be to invite the offender to accept the responsibility to make things right, to invite victims to share what is needed for restoration, and for the community to help make this possible?

Why VORP?

Victims and offenders will not experience restoration and reconciliation unless someone invites them to consider this option. VORP provides a structure that makes this possible.

In Fresno County, California, because of VORP, every day trained volunteer mediators are meeting with, inviting, and assisting victims and offenders in working through a forgiveness process. Since 1983, volunteers have worked with more than 2,500 cases.

Each time I see a victim and an offender change direction from hostility toward being more caring, I am convinced the VORP experience is a demonstration of the good news of God's reconciling spirit in action. God is interested in restoration and reconciliation with all people.

With each case, I am more convinced that if Christians only knew about VORP and how it incarnates the gospel, they would want to be involved!

Why Now?

The need is urgent. The opportunity is unprecedented.

James Rowland, recently retired director of the California Department of Corrections, is a Presbyterian and VORP volunteer. He recently told a gathering of VORP directors that criminal justice system officials describe the current situation in words like, *crisis, chaos*, and *desperation.*

He said that the truth about the present system is that we are only proving short-term public safety. Offenders are coming out of prison as fast as they are going in. With only a few exceptions, they are coming out more angry and less inclined to be productive citizens than when they went in.

Mr. Rowland volunteers with VORP because he is concerned about justice. Justice, he says, will address the needs of both the victim and the offender, and will do what is possible to encourage and bring about reconciliation. Only then will we be addressing long-term safety. Although there are many good people working for the system, he believes a power oriented punishment system simply will not address restoration and reconciliation.

A few VORP programs have been operating for several years now. Criminal justice officials have been watching. They see these programs working with a significant number of people. There is openness and interest.

Reconciliation is the work of the church. now is the time to be developing and expanding VORPs.

Why Church-Based VORP?

People of faith have been studying the biblical invitation to peacemaking and acting on this call for centuries. VORP takes forgiveness and reconciliation into an arena that is desperately in need. The church's values support VORP, and VORP offers churches an opportunity to incarnate the gospel.

Churches are in a position to provide more than just a model of an idea that then should be turned over to the state. The church is in a position to do it.

When we began VORP in Fresno County, population 550,000, officials estimated that there would be approximately 4,000 cases appropriate for VORP. At first that seemed overwhelming. But when we considered that there are more than 400 Christian churches in the county, we realized that if each provided just one volunteer mediator per month to work with one case, VORP could handle all of the cases and have mediators left over!

Because God's methods for resolving conflict work, others will be interested. Since starting VORP, I have helped introduce VORP in eleven other counties. Individuals representing many churches now provide leadership in these counties. After developing and operating VORP in your community, you will be asked to assist communities around you.

This experience is not an isolated one; VORPs in other locations are having similar experiences. We need to develop the structures to encourage and support this expansion.

Finally, it is important that we not lose sight of our source—the reconciling spirit of Jesus. Before starting a program, I would encourage you to read *VORP Organizing: A Foundation in the Church* (available from Mennonite Central Committee, 21 South 12th Street, P. O. Box 500, Akron, PA 17501-0500).

For information and technical assistance in developing a church-based VORP, write or call:

Howard Zehr   Ron Claassen
MCC Office of Criminal Justice   Center for Conflict Studies
21 South 12th Street   and Peacemaking
Box 500   1717 South Chestnut
Akron, PA 17501-0500   Fresno, CA 93702
(717) 859-1151   (202) 453-2064

Victim Offender Ministries
Mennonite Central Committee
P. O. Box 2038
Clearbrook, BC V2T 3T8
(604) 850-8734

Leader's Guide

for group study of
Justice That Heals

by Eddy Hall

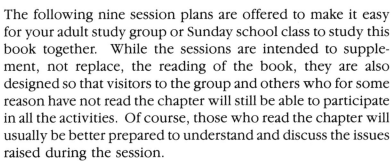

The following nine session plans are offered to make it easy for your adult study group or Sunday school class to study this book together. While the sessions are intended to supplement, not replace, the reading of the book, they are also designed so that visitors to the group and others who for some reason have not read the chapter will still be able to participate in all the activities. Of course, those who read the chapter will usually be better prepared to understand and discuss the issues raised during the session.

This study does not call for any lecturing, but rather uses a variety of discussion and sharing activities. The best leader(s) for the study, therefore, is not necessarily a gifted speaker or an expert, but rather someone who is able to stimulate discussion and guide small group processes. Because there may sometimes be strong differences of opinion on some topics, the leader(s) should also be someone who is comfortable with conflict.

The written sessions assume a study period of about forty-five minutes, but they can be shortened or expanded to fit your time available.

Preparation Alert

Leader preparation is usually simple, consisting of a careful reading of the chapter, mentally preparing for each of the learning activities, and collecting a few simple materials. For a couple of sessions, however, outside resource people or materials need to be scheduled well in advance.

Session 1—Optional: Schedule the slide-cassette dramatization *The Forgotten Neighbor* (also available on VHS videotape). Order enough copies of the companion booklet *Who Is My Neighbor?* for each group member. See Resources section following this leader's guide for descriptions of these resources and ordering information.

Session 6—If possible, arrange for one or more people who have firsthand knowledge of prison conditions to share personal experiences with the group. This could be a former inmate, a spouse of an inmate, a prison chaplain, or someone who works with a prison ministry organization enough to know several prisoners well. See session 6 instructions for details.

Optional: If it is not practical to bring in a guest to share personal experiences of prison, you may wish to schedule instead an audiovisual program that describes such an experience. See Resources section for options.

Session 7—Optional: Consider scheduling use of the slide-cassette program, *The Stanford Prison Experiment*. See Resources section for details and ordering information.

Session 8—Option 1: If a restorative justice organization works in your area, invite a staff member or volunteer to speak to your group about the work. This could, of course, include showing a video and distributing literature. Your speaker might also bring along a victim and/or offender who have been involved in the program to share about their experiences.

Option 2: Schedule a video describing the work of an organization that works with restorative justice, such as the Victim Offender Reconciliation Program or Justice Fellowship. When ordering the video, also request related literature that could be distributed to group members. *Crime: Mediating the Conflict* would be a good option. See Resources section for description and ordering information.

Session 9—If, as the study progresses, you sense that some

group members will want to follow the study with some form of tangible local involvement in restorative justice issues, invite those who show an interest to help you identify local justice-related service opportunities and to research what is being done and what could be done. To the extent that there is interest, ask these volunteers to present their findings during session 9, including specific opportunities for individuals to volunteer or for interested members of the group to join together in organizing some new initiative. Following session 5 would be a good time to begin talking to individual group members about doing such fact finding.

Optional: Invite a representative of a prison ministry or restorative justice organization to share with your group about volunteer opportunities.

SESSION 1

Who Is My Neighbor?

The Anguish of Victims

Session Objective

Help group members become more sensitive to the needs of crime victims and more willing to offer them support.

Materials Needed

Chalkboard or newsprint
Optional: Schedule the slide-cassette dramatization *The Forgotten Neighbor* (also available on VHS videotape)
Optional: Order a copy of the pamphlet *Who Is My Neighbor?* for each group member. (This accompanies *The Forgotten Neighbor*).
(Descriptions and ordering information for the above resources are found in the Resources section following this leader's guide.)

Activity 1 (12-18 min.)

Option 1: If your group has eight or more people in it, ask the members to form small groups of four to six people. Ask the group members to share in response to the following questions:

• How many of you have been victims of a crime? (This would include the murder of a family member or close friend.)

• If you are comfortable talking about it, in no more than three minutes, would you describe the crime, tell how you felt at the time, what feelings you've had about the crime since, and how you feel about it now? (Those who have been victims of more than one crime should choose just one to talk about. Those who have not been direct victims of crime should focus on trying to understand the feelings of those who have been.)

After the sharing, bring the whole group back together.

Option 2: Show the slide-cassette (or video) dramatization, *The Forgotten Neighbor*. Then invite participants to share if they have been victimized, even by minor crimes, how they felt about the experiences then, and how they feel about it now.

Activity 2 (4-6 min.)

Read the following from Isaiah 1:17: "Seek justice, encourage the oppressed" (NIV). Ask, What are some ways we can encourage those who have been oppressed by being made victims of crime?

List answers on a chalkboard or newsprint.

Activity 3 (10-15 min.)

Ask:

• Have you ever known someone who was the victim of a crime and felt like you didn't know how to support or encourage him or her? (Invite those who did not get to share during Activity 1 first opportunity to share this time.)

• Why do you think that relating to victims of crime can sometimes feel uncomfortable? (Could it be that distancing ourselves from victims is a way to distance ourselves from their pain? or to deny that it could happen to us?)

• Did any of you who have been victimized by crime experience some people keeping their distance from you? How did that feel? Were there some people who offered helpful support? What form did that support take?

Optional: Distribute copies of the pamphlet *Who Is My Neighbor?* Point out highlights of the pamphlet, particularly as they relate to the discussion you've just had concerning how best to relate to victims of crime. Encourage group members to take the pamphlets home and read them.

Activity 4 (3-5 min.)

Lead the group in a directed prayer. (You may want to have the group form a circle and hold hands.) Say:

• Do you want to offer yourself to be an "encourager of the oppressed," particularly those who have been victimized by crime? If so, would you silently offer yourself to God for that purpose?

• Would you now ask God to bring to your mind any victim

of crime to whom God might want you to offer support?

• And now would you ask God for wisdom to know what kind of support it would be helpful to offer?

• If you have any fears or anxieties about doing this, would you confess them to God? (Pause.) Offer them to God and ask for courage and peace. If fears are rooted in your own woundedness, are you willing to take steps to seek healing for that woundedness?

• Ask God to provide appropriate opportunities for you to give support and to help you know when the time is right.

Close the prayer time by aloud thanking God that you are not responsible to make everything all right for those you seek to help, but that God can touch others with love through you to bring a measure of healing.

SESSION 2

Restoration or Retribution?

The Anguish of Offenders

Session Objective

Help group members understand how a system of justice based on retribution is destructive to offenders while one based on restoration offers healing. Challenge them to support restorative justice as an expression of Christian commitment.

Materials Needed and Advance Preparation

Bibles
Chalkboard or newsprint
Paper and pencils
Before the session ask one participant to be prepared to tell the Fred Palmer story (from chapter 2) in his or her own words.

Activity 1 (5-8 min.)

Ask, How many of you know an offender who has spent time in prison? How did he or she experience the criminal justice system? Did it help to restore the offender to a productive role in society? Did it help him or her deal with any economic, social, or personal problems that contributed to the crime? Did it help to bring healing to the relationship between victim and offender? between the offender and family members? between the offender and community?

Activity 2 (6-9 min.)

Divide the group into an even number of groups of three to five people each. Each small group will need at least one Bible.

Assign half the groups to study Matthew 5:38-48. Assign the other half to study Luke 19:1-10.

Ask each group to read its passage, then to discuss: Does this passage promote a retributive (punishment-based) approach to justice or a restorative approach to justice? In what way or ways?

After three or four minutes, call the groups back together. Ask them to share their conclusions.

Activity 3 (10-15 min.)

Ask one of the participants who has read the chapter to summarize the Fred Palmer story in his or her own words. (This person should be contacted before the session to have time to prepare.) Then lead the group in discussing the questions posed by Mark Umbreit on pages 20 and 22.

Optional: If time permits, ask, What do you see as the most important differences between retributive and restorative justice? (The chapter lists several contrasts.) Make two columns on a chalkboard or newsprint, one headed "Retributive justice," the other "Restorative justice." Summarize the answers in the appropriate columns.

Activity 4 (12-20 min.)

Tell your group, "Imagine that our city council has realized that its punishment-based approach to crime is counterproductive and too expensive. They have assembled a study group to explore and recommend restorative alternatives. We are that group."

Distribute paper and pencils to each participant, and ask participants to form pairs. As the first step in this process, tell them they are to list as many answers to this question as they can think of in three minutes: "What are the negative effects of a punishment-based approach to crime that our alternatives should seek to correct?"

After you call time, have each pair join with another pair, forming groups of four. (If you have an odd number of pairs, you may get one group of six.) As the second step in this process, ask these groups to brainstorm alternatives to punitive approaches to justice that would avoid the problems they have listed during the first step. Allow six to eight minutes, depending on how much time you have available.

Finally, call the whole group back together and have the groups report. Use the chalkboard or newsprint to compile the best ideas of each group into an overall master plan to be presented to the "city council." You can take anywhere from three to ten minutes for this part of the activity, depending on time available.

If you have an imaginative class, this activity could provide an exciting opportunity to come up with creative alternatives they have never before considered.

Close with prayer, asking God to help you to envision more creative, restorative responses to offenders, rooted in the teachings and actions of Jesus.

SESSION 3

From Eye for Eye to Steadfast Love

Justice in the Old Testament

Session Objective

Help participants see that God's revelation through the Old Testament progressively called people away from vengeance and toward restoration.

Materials Needed

One copy of Agree-Disagree survey for each participant. (Each participant may use the copy (p. 165) in his or her book, or you can make photocopies.)

Pencils

Bibles

Activity 1 (6-10 min.)

Provide each participant with a pencil and a copy of the Agree-Disagree survey on page 165. Make Bibles available for those who wish to look up reference verses. Allow a minute or so for them to circle their answers.

Lead the group in discussing these five statements. Keep in mind the purposes of this activity—to engage the group in this session's topic, and to focus some of the issues involved in an Old Testament study of justice. Since this activity is designed to raise questions and pique interest, do not try to bring resolution on any of the five issues where there is disagreement. Rather, move on to the next statement while there is still a lack of resolution. The lack of resolution is intended to provide motivation for the Bible study which follows. (Resolution can come later in the session.)

Activity 2 (10-15 min.)

Divide into four teams. (If you have fewer than eight people, divide into two teams, and give each team two assignments.) Each team will need at least one Bible. From the section of chapter 3 headed "God's Justice Versus Society's Justice," assign each of the following topics to a team: unlimited retaliation, limited retaliation, limited love, unlimited love. (If you have only two teams, assign the first two topics to one team, the last two to the other.)

Direct each team to do the following:

1. Read the part of chapter 3 that explains the term you have been assigned. (The team studying "unlimited love" should also skim the final section of the chapter for parts related to their topic.)

2. Try to think of examples of your term ("unlimited retaliation," etc.), at least one example from Scripture and one from history or current events.

After three to five minutes, while the teams remain seated together, ask each team in turn to share examples of its term, including those given in the chapter.

Before calling on each team, briefly introduce the term to provide continuity between the terms, so the group will understand the historical sequence in God's dealing with people from unlimited retaliation (humanity's natural sinful response) to limited retaliation to limited love to unlimited love.

This activity is the heart of the lesson. If questions arise that bear directly on the topic of justice in the Old Testament, take time to discuss them.

Conclude this activity by asking, Which of these four standards, on the scale from unlimited retaliation to unlimited love, does Jesus call us to live by in the New Testament?

Activity 3 (12-18 min.)

As an exercise in applying these terms to contemporary events, give each team one more assignment: "Imagine that you belong to a country that makes the principle you studied (for example, limited retaliation) the basis of its international relations. Give your country a fictitious name, then together decide what a foreign policy built on this principle would look like. Things you might look at could include level of defense spending, trade policies, foreign aid (what kind and how much), international decision-making procedures, the basis for international alliances, ways of responding to economic threats (such as loss of access to a nation's oil fields), ways of responding to military threats, spending priorities, and policies toward foreigners living within the country."

After five to eight minutes (depending on time available), invite each team to share how its foreign policy shaped up.

In leading discussion on this activity, keep in mind that the purpose of the activity is to help participants better understand the four principles by applying them to contemporary situations, not to come to agreement on what kind of foreign policy is most Christian. (That may be an important issue, but it's outside the scope of this book.)

One question likely to arise is whether a foreign policy based on unlimited love could really work. (Your team imagining what this might look like may or may not decide that this would involve a commitment to nonviolence.) If any group members are interested in further exploring the practical possibilities of nonviolent resistance as an alternative to government-sponsored violence, you might refer them to Ronald J. Sider's book, *Nonviolence, The Invincible Weapon?* (Word, 1989).

Activity 4 (4-8 min.)

Bring the whole group back together. Ask, How, if at all, has your view of God's justice in the Old Testament changed as a result of reading this chapter or of participating in today's session? You might also ask if any participants would now respond differently to any of the Agree/Disagree statements than they did at the beginning of the session.

Close with a prayer asking God to renew your minds by replacing society's ideas of justice with God's ideas of justice, and giving the compassion and courage to be faithful to God's ideals.

SESSION 4

A Wideness in God's Mercy
Justice in the New Testament

Session Objective

Encourage participants, on the basis of New Testament teaching, to respond to offenders not on the basis of what they deserve, but on the basis of what they need.

Materials Needed

Chalkboard or newsprint
Bibles

Activity 1 (4-6 min.)

Open your session by trying to spark a debate between participants. Write the following two descriptions of justice on a chalkboard or newsprint, and ask participants to indicate by show of hands which description they feel better expresses the idea of justice.

Description #1: Justice is done when a person gets what he or she deserves.

Description #2: Justice is done when a person gets what he or she needs to be helped back toward wholeness and right relationships.

After participants have raised their hands, ask people to explain why they chose their answers. If there is too much unanimity (for example, if most of the class chooses description #2), be prepared to play devil's advocate. You could say, for example, "Maybe you voted for #2 because you feel that is what we as Christians are called to do. But just because we're called to do it doesn't make it justice. Isn't that a definition of grace rather than justice?"

Of course, the truth is that both descriptions are accurate descriptions of justice. It's just that they describe different kinds of justice. Description #1 is of retributive justice. Description #2 is of restorative justice. And, yes, mercy (not getting the punishment we deserve) is an essential aspect of restorative justice, because often getting the punishment we deserve would have a destructive rather than restorative effect on us and our relationships. Add the labels "RETRIBUTIVE JUSTICE" and "RESTORATIVE JUSTICE" to the descriptions on the chalkboard or newsprint.

Activity 2 (10-15 min.)

Distribute Bibles and ask various participants to read the following passages. After each is read, ask, Is this an example of retributive justice or restorative justice?
• Romans 2:5-6 (retributive)
• Luke 7:36-50 (restorative)
• 2 Thessalonians 1:5-6 (retributive)
• Luke 19:1-10 (restorative)
• John 7:53—8:11 (restorative)
Next have someone read Romans 12:19-21. Ask:
• According to this passage, when is it appropriate for Christians to exercise retributive justice? (Never. God reserves retributive justice to himself. Note that the examples of retributive justice in Romans and 2 Thessalonians referred to God's judgment, not to Christians exercising judgment.)
• What parts of this Romans passage describe restorative justice? (Verses 20 and 21. In effect, in this passage Paul is saying, "Do not exercise retributive justice, but leave that to God; instead, exercise restorative justice.")
• Is punishment always inconsistent with restorative justice? (By this point in the discussion some people may be getting the idea that restorative justice means that offenders are to be allowed to continue their destructive behavior without correction. This question focuses on the need for correction as a part of restoration. You might have a group member read 2 Corinthians 2:5-11 and 2 Thessalonians 3:14-15 for examples of punishment that have a restorative purpose. Discuss the difference between retributive justice and punishment as one component of restorative justice. Is motive—revenge versus love for the offender—the only difference, or are there practical differences in whether, how, and

for how long punishment is administered?)

Optional: Ask someone to read from chapter 4 the quote from Thomas Yoder Neufeld on page 45.

Activity 3 (10-15 min.)

Form groups of about four. Ask each group member to think of a time he or she received mercy. This could be any occasion of receiving forgiveness from God or from another person. It could be the forgiving of a financial debt. It could be a story of another person repaying evil or injury, not with revenge or demand of payment, but with an offer of help. Invite all who feel comfortable doing so to share their stories with their groups.

After several minutes, as the sharing seems to be winding down, ask the group members to consider how their stories might have been different if the person or persons they wronged had responded not with mercy, but with retributive justice—demanding that they pay the full price for their wrongs. What effect might that have had on them? Ask them at the same time to share if they feel the merciful response they received had a healing or restorative effect in their lives. If so, how?

If time permits, ask the groups to share in response to one more question: How can you apply the distinction between retributive and restorative justice in your day-to-day relationships? What difference might it make in your responses if whenever you are wronged you consciously seek to respond restoratively rather than retributively? If people seem to need help getting started on this one, suggest they consider parent-child relationships, marriage relationships, hurts caused by friends or relatives, or conflicts within the church.

Activity 4 (4-6 min.)

Bring the whole group back together. Ask participants to close their eyes and to think of two shameful things they have done in their lives. Then ask them to imagine what price they would have had to pay if God had punished them as they deserved to be punished for their wrongs.

While group members still have their eyes closed, read the

quote from Clarence Jordan and Bill Lane Doulos found in the Aids to Reflection at the end of chapter 4 (pages 50-51).

Explain that in the Lord's Prayer, the "as" in the phrase "Forgive us our debts as we forgive our debtors" means "in the same measure as" or "to the same degree that." Therefore, when we pray the Lord's Prayer, we are asking God to grant or withhold forgiveness to the same degree that we grant or withhold forgiveness in relation to those who have wronged us.

Close by praying the Lord's Prayer in unison. Form a circle and hold hands for the prayer if that is appropriate for your group.

SESSION 5

What's So Good About Blind Justice?

The Purpose of Law

Session Objective

Help participants understand the incompatibility between the purposes of secular laws and God's law; show them why secular courts (from God's perspective) cannot help but be unjust; and encourage them to explore alternatives to secular courts.

Materials Needed

Chalkboard or newsprint
Bibles

Activity 1 (8-12 min.)

Write on a chalkboard or newsprint the heading, "THE PURPOSES OF LAW." Ask group members to list as many purposes of law as they can think of. Jot down their answers below the heading.

When your list is finished, ask, Do you feel the governmental laws we live under today have the same purposes as the laws of the Old Testament—Israel's laws—or are there some differences in purpose? As part of the discussion of this question, ask a group member to read the first four paragraphs of the section of chapter 5 headed "The Letter or the Spirit of the Law?" (ending with footnote 5). To help participants internalize this information, you may then want to ask: According to the author, how is the purpose of Torah, or Old Testament law, different from the purpose of contemporary governmental law?

Activity 2 (8-12 min.)

Distribute Bibles. Have the participants form groups of four or five. Assign half of the groups to study Deuteronomy 22:22-

24 and John 7:53—8:11. Assign the other half to study Exodus 20:8-11 and Mark 2:23—3:6. The questions the groups are to answer are: From these stories, what can we learn about how Jesus understood law? Are Jesus' actions in these stories consistent with his words in Matthew 5:17?

After five minutes or so, ask the groups to report, summarizing the passages they read and the answers they came up with. It may be appropriate during this discussion to mention or ask someone to read Romans 13:10 ("love is the fulfilling of the law") or 2 Corinthians 3:6 ("the letter kills, but the Spirit gives life").

Wrap up the Bible study by relating the discussion to the conclusion of Activity 1: that Jesus did not understand the law as a rigid set of rules to be objectively applied (blind justice), but as principles to guide toward healing and restoration. Therefore he consistently gave priority to the intent of the law over the literal application of the law, and in so doing he fulfilled the law. In contrast, Jesus sharply condemns those who meticulously obey the letter of the law while ignoring its spirit or purpose (see Matthew 5:20).

Activity 3 (12-15 min.)

Ask a volunteer to read the last three paragraphs of the section of chapter 5 headed "Retaliation or Restoration?", beginning with "The Bible is deeply suspicious...."

After the passage is read, highlight the author's main point: Secular courts are by their very nature unjust, from a Christian perspective, because their understanding of justice is not based on the gospel. The purpose of secular law is to retaliate against the lawbreaker; the purpose of God's law and the gospel is to promote peace and the possibility of reconciliation.

Ask a volunteer to read 1 Corinthians 6:1-8.

Pose the question: If secular courts make decisions based on principles contrary to God's justice, should Christians seek alternative ways to resolve disputes that in our society are normally handled by the courts? Perhaps some group members will share from their own experience examples of situations normally settled in court that they have been able to handle outside of court in a way that promoted healing and reconciliation. If no such stories are forthcoming, read one or both of the following case studies. Ask the group to propose possible courses of action, then to suggest which one holds the greatest promise of healing and reconciliation.

Case Study 1 (a slightly disguised actual case)

At a school-sponsored social event, Jackie, another parent with whom you are acquainted but don't know well, mentions a discipline problem she is having with her four-year-old son. She says that about once a week she has to "beat him"—her phrase—with a paddle, and that it turns his bottom black with bruises. The boy will then be sweet for a few days and feel very close to her. A week later when his behavior gets out of control, she repeats the beating. She goes on to say that she knows this is how she is to discipline her son, because God has told her to do this.

About all you know about Jackie is that she has very poor social skills and that she goes to church in a nearby town. You consider calling Child Protective Services asking them to investigate for child abuse. You hesitate, however, because of your previous experience with Protective Services social workers. They often remove the child from the home first, then ask questions later. Rather than actively working for reconciliation, they tend to treat the abusive parents as adversaries and seek to limit or even terminate the relationship between parent and child. Such cases may be in the courts for years, and often result in fragmentation of the family, including divorce.

In discussing what Jackie has said with friends of yours who know her better, you find that there is no reason to suspect that she would be lying or exaggerating to get attention—she is scrupulously honest. You feel, rather, that her telling you about the beatings is likely an unconscious cry for help.

You and your spouse consider following the procedure of Matthew 18:15-17, but hesitate, feeling that your limited acquaintance with Jackie hardly gives you the relational basis or spiritual authority to initiate such a confrontation. Matthew 18, you feel, is to be implemented within the context of a covenant Christian community.

Should you move ahead with Matthew 18 anyway, in spite of not having a significant relationship with her? What other alternatives do you have? Which alternative do you think would hold out the greatest possibility for achieving God's purposes of healing, restoration, and reconciliation? Might it be necessary to involve Protective Services simultaneously with alternate approaches since only Protective Services would have legal authority to remove the child from the home if that became necessary?

If you had discovered the abuse in your capacity as a school-teacher or health professional, so that you were required by law to report the abuse to legal authorities, would that make a difference in how you chose to respond? If you felt an alternative approach to the problem held out greater prospect of bringing restoration and reconciliation, would you take the risks associated with breaking the letter of the law for the sake of fulfilling its spirit?

Case Study 2

For two years you have been in a business partnership with Carl, who attends a church of another denomination. One day, without warning, he cleans out the partnership bank account and moves away. Not only does Carl take all the partnership's cash, but he leaves you with sizable business debts that you by yourself don't have the resources to pay. You reach Carl by phone to confront him, and he warns you not to tell any creditors to come to him for payment, or he'll simply file for bankruptcy.

What are your options? Which option do you feel holds out the greatest promise of restoration and reconciliation?

Activity 4 (3-6 min.)

Ask, Are there situations involving human hurt in our community that are being processed through the "blind justice" of secular courts that could be more redemptively handled through the church or a church-related agency committed to healing and restoration?

While discussing such situations and what can be done

about them could obviously fill an entire class session or more, the purpose of this closing activity is simply to encourage participants to consider whether today's session can have practical application in your community. If some group members show an interest in pursuing this further, see the suggestion for After the Session below.

Conclude by recapping the fundamental difference between the purposes of biblical law and contemporary governmental law. Most contemporary governmental law is adversarial—one party wins and the other loses. The process usually brings further alienation and injury. In contrast, the goal of biblical justice is, so far as possible, to heal the injury and restore the broken relationships caused by the offense, with equal concern for doing what is best for both victims and offenders. God calls us all to respond to offense with these redemptive goals, not with revenge or retaliation.

Announcement

Session 6 is optional, depending on whether you have available the resource person or persons to come in for the session. If you are not using session 6, at the end of session 5, announce to your group that they should read both chapters 6 and 7 in preparation for your next session.

After the Session

By now you should be beginning to get a feel for whether members of your group are likely to want to translate what they are learning into some kind of local justice-related service. If one or more group members already show interest in at least exploring options, talk with them outside of group sessions to learn more of their interests, encourage them to gather more information about the situations they are personally interested in, and to be prepared to share what they have learned in session 9. See session 9 instructions for ideas on how to direct your volunteers' information gathering.

SESSION 6

Am I My Brother's Jailkeeper?

A Critique of Imprisonment

This Session Optional

Chapters 6 and 7 are about imprisonment and its alternatives. The two chapters can be studied together, using session 7 of the leader's guide. This session is included as an optional session for those groups that have access to a resource person who can share from personal experience about the effects of imprisonment on inmates, or a similar audiovisual presentation.

Session Objective

Raise group members' consciousness of the dehumanizing effect of imprisonment and the failure of prisons to rehabilitate offenders.

Advance Preparation

Option 1: Several weeks before the session, arrange for a former inmate, an inmate's spouse, a prison chaplain, or someone who does regular volunteer work with prisoners to visit your group and share from personal experience. Your guest may either speak, following guidelines you provide, or you or another person may interview your guest. Which approach you follow will depend on what your guest feels more comfortable with, and whether you feel your guest needs to be guided by interview questions to be sure of addressing the points you wish to cover. In either case, plan to leave some time at the end of the session for your guest to answer questions from the group.

Option 2: Schedule an audiovisual presentation on the topic of how imprisonment affects prisoners. (See Resources section for options.)

Activity 1 (entire session)

Option 1—Guest speaker/interviewee—Introduce your guest, briefly describing how he or she has related to the prison system. If your guest is a former inmate or the spouse of an inmate, everyone will be wondering what the person is charged with or has been convicted of, and how long the person served in prison. It may be less awkward for you to mention these things matter-of-factly in your introduction rather than leaving it to your guest to answer those questions. The purpose for your guest's visit is to describe not his or her crime, but the prison experience and its effect on him or her. Keep that focus clearly in mind throughout the session.

The following questions can serve either as interview questions, or as possible points for your guest to use in a prepared talk. Each question is related to a section of the chapter. You will want to carefully study the chapter in relation to these questions so you'll understand what each question is driving at and be prepared to ask follow-up or clarifying questions as appropriate.

1. Crucial to making a successful fresh start upon leaving prison is having healthy *self-esteem*. Would you say that imprisonment contributes to improved self-esteem or lower self-esteem? What are some specific circumstances or ways of being treated that contribute to lower self-esteem? What circumstances or relationships contribute to strong self-esteem?

2. Many people are in prison because of an inappropriate reliance on violence. Does prison teach inmates to be less violent or more violent? In what ways? Have you observed the attitudes of nonviolent offenders toward violence change during their imprisonment? If so, in what ways?

3. A key to succeeding after imprisonment is to nurture healthy relationships—with family members, friends, co-workers. How much opportunity is there in prison to develop skills for caring relationships? Or does the prison experience tend toward teaching inmates to relate based on domination? Can you give examples?

4. Experts agree that basic family relationships are crucial

to rehabilitation. What effects does imprisonment have on family relationships?

5. Another skill critical to success upon completion of a prison term is the ability to make good personal decisions. How much opportunity is there in the prison setting to develop skills in being self-governing?

6. From your observation, do you feel prisons are doing an effective job of rehabilitating offenders? Are most inmates better prepared or less well prepared to face life after completing a prison sentence? more or less likely to stay out of trouble with the law? What explanations can you offer for your observations?

7. If you had the power to change the prison system, or even to replace it with something different, what changes would you make? Why?

If your guest is a Christian who has served time, it would also be appropriate to invite him or her to briefly share how he or she experienced God's grace in prison.

Following the talk or interview, invite group members to ask your guest questions. Make sure your guest feels free to not answer any questions he or she would prefer not to answer.

Close your session with prayer. Your prayer can touch on the prison system and those who are victims of the system, both inmates and staff. Especially if your guest is a former inmate, it may be appropriate to gather around your guest to pray for God's blessing on his or her new start in life.

Option 2—Audiovisual—Though this will probably be less powerful than a guest speaker, an audiovisual program can be a good second choice for how to handle this session. After showing the audiovisual, lead the class in discussing the same questions listed under option 1, with group members drawing on what they have learned from reading the chapter and from the audiovisual to answer the questions.

After the Session

If your guest was a former inmate or the spouse of an inmate, next week you may want to consider as a group whether you would like to provide some form of continuing support to the family. If the family does not already have a church family, of course, you could invite them to be a part of yours. You might sensitively check into needs—financial, educational, employment, child care, transportation, health care, counseling. Don't overlook, however, the most basic need of all—for friends who care.

If your guest is a chaplain or someone who works with a prison ministry, you or another group member may want to explore ways individuals or a group from the church could become involved in ministry to prisoners. Be alert to those who show such interest and speak to them after the session, requesting that they get more details about ministry opportunities and be prepared to share them during session 9.

SESSION 7

Can Prisons Be Made to Work?

Humanizing Imprisonment, Creating Alternatives

Session Objective

Make participants aware of steps that can and are being taken to make prisons less dehumanizing, but also of the need to create and use alternatives to prison because of a retributive system's inability to achieve restoration.

Materials Needed and Advance Preparation

Pencils and paper
Optional: Schedule the slide-cassette presentation *The Stanford Prison Experiment*. (See Resources section for description and ordering information.)

Activity 1 (10-12 min.)

Form two groups of no more than five or six. If you have more than twelve participants, form more groups.

Ask each group to discuss what problems in prisons most urgently need reform to make the prisons less dehumanizing. Give each group two or three minutes to agree on five problems to list on its paper.

When time is up, have the groups exchange papers. Each group then is to come up with a program of prison reforms that addresses each of the problems listed on the paper it has just been handed. Allow groups six to eight minutes to work. Then ask them to report on what they came up with.

Activity 2 (16-20 min.)

Option 1—Debate—This activity is a debate on the question: Can prisons be made to work?

Divide the class into two working groups. Group 1 should prepare to take the affirmative, making the case that with the right reforms, the prison system can be made to work, to bring healing and restoration to offenders. To make their case, this group should propose a program of reforms that they feel would accomplish this goal.

Group 2 should prepare to take the negative, making the case that the nature of imprisonment so damages the human spirit that the possible benefits of even well-intentioned rehabilitation programs are more than offset by the destructive effects of the prison environment.

In instructing each group, point out that even if some group members are not personally convinced of the position they are asked to advocate, they should still try to make the strongest possible case for their assigned point of view.

Each group should select two debaters, one to make a two- to three-minute presentation of the case developed by the group, and one to make a one-minute rebuttal of the other side's case.

Give the sides about five or six minutes to develop their cases. Then ask the debaters to make their presentations as follows:

First affirmative—two to three minutes
First negative—two to three minutes
Second affirmative (rebuttal)—one minute
Second negative (rebuttal)—one minute

Of course, the point of all this isn't to win the debate, but to stimulate and clarify thinking about the issues on both sides of the argument.

Option 2—Audiovisual—Show the slide-cassette presentation *The Stanford Prison Experiment*. After the presentation, lead the class in discussing it. Ask what it reveals about the effects of the prison structure on both prisoners and keepers. What does this suggest about the usefulness of prison as a rehabilitative or restorative structure?

Activity 3 (10-20 min.)

Divide into groups of four or five, making sure a recorder in each group has pencil and paper. Announce the following assignment to the groups:

I want you to imagine that our state or province is seriously interested in changing our so-called corrections system over from a retributive system to a restorative system. Rather than determining to "make criminals pay," the government wants to come up with a corrections system that will help make offenders productive members of society. This new system is to respond to the needs of victims in a serious, dignified way that will lead toward healing.

Your group is a task force charged with designing a new system that will accomplish these goals as effectively as possible. Your plan may incorporate any number of alternative ways of meeting the needs of victims, and of holding offenders accountable and helping them become more productive citizens.

The government is assuming that as a part of this plan, from 80 to 100 percent of the prison space will no longer be needed, and the funds freed up from operating the closed prisons will be available to fund your alternative programs. What kind of programs will you recommend?

Allow the groups to work on their plans up until about five or six minutes before the end of the period, then ask them to report what they came up with. You might close by asking, If your plans could be implemented, do you think they would really have a chance of working? Why or why not?

SESSION 8

Liberty to the Captives

Restorative Responses to Victims and Offenders

Session Objective

Increase participants' awareness of models of response to victims and offenders that help to restore and reconcile.

Materials Needed and Advance Preparation

Chalkboard or newsprint

Optional: If a restorative justice organization works in your area, invite a staff member or volunteer to speak to your group about the work. See Activity 2, option 1, for details.

Optional: If a speaker is not available, consider ordering a video describing the work of a restorative justice organization such as the Victim Offender Reconciliation Program or Justice Fellowship. When ordering the video, request related literature for distribution. *Crime: Mediating the Victim Offender Conflict* would be a good option. (See Resources section for description and ordering information.)

Activity 1 (2 min.)

Ask: Do victims and offenders need each other? Why or why not? Don't try to bring consensus on this question at this point. The purpose of this question is simply to create interest and focus on the session's topic. You'll return to this question in a different form at the end of the session.

Activity 2 (15-40 min.)

Option 1—Guest speaker/interviewee—If you are able to get a speaker from a restorative justice organization to describe his or her work with the organization, devote the bulk of your session to your speaker. If a victim and offender who have been served by the organization can also come and share their experiences, so much the better. The speaker may also wish to show a short video or distribute literature to introduce the work of the organization to the group.

Try to allow time for group members to ask your guest(s) questions about their experiences.

Option 2—Audiovisual—Schedule an audiovisual program that demonstrates a model for victims and offenders working together to achieve reconciliation. *Crime: Mediating the Victim Offender Conflict* is an option. After the presentation, ask the group:

• How does this model address needs of victims?
• How does this model address needs of offenders?

Distribute or make available any literature that came with the program.

This option can be combined with option 3.

Option 3—Case studies—Form groups of three or four persons. Assign half the groups to look at the case study in chapter 8 described under the heading, "Case Study: Victim Offender Reconciliation Group." Assign the other half to look at the story in the two paragraphs immediately preceding that case study—the story of the young man who broke into a daycare center.

Each group is to read its assigned story to find answers to these two questions: How did this process address the needs of victims? How did this process address the needs of offenders?

After four or five minutes, ask the groups to report, first by summarizing their stories, then by sharing their conclusions about how the process met the needs of the parties involved.

This option could be combined with option 2.

Activity 3 (5-7 min.)

Ask:

• In light of what we've learned since the beginning of the session, we should be ready to answer more confidently the question of whether victims and offenders need each other.

Make two columns on the chalkboard or newsprint. Head the first "WHAT VICTIMS NEED FROM OFFENDERS" and the second "WHAT OFFENDERS NEED FROM VICTIMS." As group members name what victims and offenders need from each other, list their answers.

Activity 4 (3-5 min.)

If time permits, invite participants to reflect on any damaged personal relationships they have. Even though no crime may be involved, ask them to silently reflect on how the list your group has just generated might apply to that relationship. You might say, for example:

• As an injured party, do you need some of the same things from the person who hurt you that victims need from offenders in our list?

• As one who has hurt another, do you need some of the same things from the person you hurt as offenders need from their victims in the list?

• Would it be useful for you to invite a mediator to help you and this other person to work with you in resolving your conflict? Or is it something you can work out one-on-one?

• Do you see anything in the victim-offender reconciliation process that you might be able to use to help heal a damaged personal relationship you have with another person?

These questions might be followed with a minute or so of silence for reflection and prayer. Close the session with conversational prayer if your group is familiar with and comfortable with it.

SESSION 9

The Restorative Justice Vision
What Can Christians Do?

Session Objective

Invite participants to consider how they can personally become part of carrying out the restorative justice vision.

Materials Needed and Advance Preparation

Optional: Three or four weeks before this session, identify group members outside who show some interest in researching or becoming personally involved in restorative justice. Ask them to gather information about the particular program or area they are most interested in and be prepared to present it to the group during this session. If possible, such presentations should include opportunities for volunteer involvement. Optional: Invite a representative of a prison ministry or restorative justice organization to share with your group about volunteer opportunities.
Optional: Bring to class a stack of newspapers that includes numerous stories related to crime and punishment, preferably including papers published by different publishers.

Planning the Session

This closing session can follow either of two lesson plans. You will need to decide which is more appropriate to your group depending on whether you sense you have group members interested in exploring active local involvement in restorative justice issues. If you do, you should follow Plan #1. If you feel you do not, Plan #2 will probably be more appropriate.

Lesson Plan #1

Activity 1 (30-35 min.)

   Devote most of this session to informing your group about opportunities to become personally involved in restorative justice work and giving them opportunity to respond. You will need to tailor this session to your situation. Possible elements include:

• Allowing class members who have researched local involvement opportunities to present the information they have gathered. This could include reporting on conversations, distributing literature, or showing a display or audiovisual program about a local organization or ministry. This could even include scheduling a group visit to a prison or agency office for those who wish to further explore the possibility of volunteering.

• Inviting a representative of a prison ministry or restorative justice organization to talk about volunteer opportunities— the time involved, the training available, and so on. This too could include scheduling a follow-up meeting for those interested in exploring further.

• If a member of the group has really been captured by this vision, he or she might even make a presentation on how to organize a Victim Offender Reconciliation Program or some similar program that interests him or her. This would be an opportunity to gauge if there are enough interested people to form a core group to start such a ministry.

Activity 2 (6-10 min.)

Ask the class to read and consider Will Campbell's suggestions in chapter 9 that each congregation "adopt" just one person who is released from prison, offering fellowship and support. And that each congregation "adopt" just one prisoner, visiting him or her each week, bringing word from the free world to the prison, returning to the congregation with word from prison. Discuss:

• Are Campbell's suggestions realistic?

• Are they within the reach of your congregation?

• If you wanted to implement Campbell's suggestions, what would it take?

• How would you identify your prisoner and ex-prisoner to "adopt"? Is this something you would like to further explore as a congregation? If so, who will take responsibility for following through with the exploration?

Ask if there are ways your congregation could minister more effectively to victims. How could you further explore those options?

Close with prayer.

Lesson Plan #2

Activity 1 (10-15 min.)

Have group members form pairs. Pass out newspapers—one per pair. Have people look through the papers, tearing out articles about crime, prisons, and related topics.

Next have two pairs join together so that you have groups of four. Using Eleanor MacLean's checklist from chapter 9 (under the heading "Analyzing the Media's Treatment of Crime"), analyze the two articles. The bottom line, of course, is to determine what bias the writer brings to the story.

After several minutes, invite class members to share their stories with the class. Each person reporting should briefly summarize the news story, then tell what bias, if any, the writer seems to have, and how that bias is evident.

Ask: How important is it to learn to read between the lines— spot reporter bias—when reading newspaper accounts of crime? Does it make any practical difference in anything?

Activity 2 (8-15 min.)

Ask the class to read and consider Will Campbell's suggestions on page 110 that each congregation "adopt" just one person who is released from prison, offering fellowship and support. And that each congregation "adopt" just one prisoner, visiting him or her each week, bringing word from the free world to the prison, returning to the congregation with word from prison. Discuss:

• Are Campbell's suggestions realistic?

• Are they within the reach of your congregation?

• If you wanted to implement Campbell's suggestions, what would it take?

• How would you identify your prisoner and ex-prisoner to "adopt"? Is this something you would like to further explore as a congregation? If so, who will take responsibility for following through with the exploration?

Ask if there are ways your congregation could minister more effectively to victims. How could you further explore those options?

Activity 3 (10-20 min.)

Use this time to wrap up your study. Ask group members to share:

• What has most surprised you during this study?

• What has most bothered you?

• How, if at all, do you expect your actions to change as a result of what you've learned?

Close with conversational prayer.

Resources

compiled by Wayne Northey and Howard Zehr

Many of the resources listed on these pages are available from your local library or bookstore.

These resources are also available from the two Mennonite Central Committee offices listed here. Resource lists are available upon request. Also available is "Biblical/Theological Works Contributing to Restorative Justice: A Bibliographic Essay" by Wayne Northey. It does exactly what the title indicates.

Write, telephone or FAX:

Victim Offender Ministries   Information Services
Mennonite Central   Mennonite Central Committee
Committee Canada   21 S. 12th, P.O. Box 500
P.O. Box 2038   Akron, PA 17501-0500
Clearbrook, BC V2T 3T8   Telephone (717) 859-1151
Telephone (604) 850-6639   FAX (717) 859-2171
FAX (604) 850-8734

Additional resource lists are available from the U.S. Association for Victim Offender Mediation, c/o PACT, 254 S. Morgan Blvd., Valparaiso, IN 46383; telephone (219) 462-1127.

Chapter 1

Print
Christian:
   Who Is My Neighbor? by Howard Zehr is designed to help

congregations and other groups discover practical ways of reaching out to victims. 15pp. Companion slide set/VHS video is also available. Order from Mennonite Central Committee, 21 South 12th Street, P.O. Box 500, Akron, PA 17501-0500. $.25 each.

The Christian as Victim by Howard Zehr, with sections by Dave Jackson, examines the experience of victimization and discusses how Christians could respond when victimized. Order from Mennonite Central Committee, 21 South 12th Street, P.O. Box 500, Akron, PA 17501-0500. $.40 each.

Secular:

Victims: The Orphans of Justice by Jerry Armenic, Seal Books, McClelland and Stewart-Bantam Limited, Toronto, Ont., 1984. It is a ringing denunciation of a justice system perceived by victims to be more attuned to the criminal than the victim, and certainly not responsive to victims' needs.

What Murder Leaves Behind: The Victim's Family by Doug Magee, Dodd, Mead & Company, New York, 1983. Portraits and interviews focusing attention on the social, psychological, and legal consequences of violent crime on victims' families. Sensitively done.

Audiovisual

The Forgotten Neighbor (slide-tape set, also part of a VHS video, including *Crime: the Broken Community*, and *Crime: Mediating the Conflict*) explores a crime victim's needs and suggests some appropriate responses by the church. This resource goes along with the *Who Is My Neighbor?* booklet. Order from Mennonite Central Committee, 21 South 12th Street, P.O. Box 500, Akron, PA 17501-0500. Loan at no charge or purchase for $15.

Chapter 2

Print

Christian (see also resources for chapters 6 and 8):

Crime and Its Victims: What We Can Do by Daniel W. Van Ness, InterVarsity Press, Downers Grove, Illinois, 1986. The author offers much practical help in seeing crime primarily as a person-to-person phenomenon, to be addressed as such, as opposed to the traditional understanding that crime primarily is a violation against the state.

Crime and Reconciliation: Creative Options for Victims and Offenders by Mark Umbreit, Abingdon Press, Nashville, 1985. It points to a restorative model of justice through case studies, biblical material, and stories.

Secular:

Justice Without Law? by Jerold Auerbach, Oxford University Press, New York, 1983. Demonstrates the American roots of informal justice systems in America and discusses the pros and cons of moving to a wider system of informal justice.

Informal Justice? ed. by Roger Matthews, SAGE Publications, London, 1988. Informal justice such as mediation, arbitration, conciliation, and reparation arose out of attempts to take disputes out of the formal, legal process and restore them to the community. An evaluation is given to test the benefits of informal justice to victims, offenders, and the criminal justice system. Some articles are fairly technical.

Justice for Victims and Offenders by Martin Wright, Open University Press, Milton Keynes, Philadelphia, 1991. Examines the theory and failure of criminal law and argues for a restorative justice model.

Audiovisual

Crime: The Broken Community (slide set and part of VHS video, including *The Forgotten Neighbor* and *Crime: Mediating the Conflict*) looks briefly (12 min.) at the criminal justice process from the points of view of the victim, the offender, the judge, and the Bible. It stresses the need for new alternatives which allow for restitution and repair. This audiovisual is designed to be a starting point for discussions about alternatives, the church's involvement in criminal justice, and VORP (Victim Offender Reconciliation Program). Order from Mennonite Central Committee, 21 South 12th Street, P.O. Box 500, Akron, PA 17501-0500. Loan at no charge or purchase for $15.

Chapter 3

Print

Monotheism, Power, Justice: Collected Old Testament Essays by Millard C. Lind, Text Reader Series No. 3, Institute of Mennonite Studies, Elkhart, Ind., 1990. Most applicable to the study of chapter 3 is Section II, "Law, Justice and Power," especially the essay, "Transformation of Justice: From Moses to Jesus." (This essay is also available as New Perspectives on Crime and Justice: Occasional Paper No. 5 from Mennonite Central Committee. Order from Mennonite Central Committee, 21 South 12th Street, P.O. Box 500, Akron, PA 17501-0500. $1.00 single copy, $.40 multiple copies.) The author argues that God's way always is antithetical to the way of state institutionalized violence. He contends that the Old Testament is one continuous NO to state law in favor of covenant law which at its heart is mercy. Order from Institute of Mennonite Studies, 3003 Benham Ave., Elkhart, IN 46517.

Old Testament Law by Dale Patrick, John Knox Press, 1985. The last three chapters, and epilogue, are the most important of a work which discerns a consistent emphasis in both Testaments of spirit over letter. The spirit of the law is ever love, supremely seen in the self-emptying, self-giving of the incarnation.

The Death Penalty Debate by H. Wayne House and John H. Yoder, Word Publishing, Dallas, Texas, 1991. The biblical material relevant to the death penalty is the focus of this debate. The discussion includes examination of biblical perspectives on retribution.

A Biblical Vision of Justice by Herman Bianchi and *More Justice, Less Law* by John Pendleton are small booklets in the New Perspectives on Crime and Justice: Occasional Papers series by Mennonite Central Committee. Order from Mennonite Central Committee, 21 South 12th Street, P.O. Box 500, Akron, PA 17501-0500. $1.00 single copies; $.40 multiple copies.

Audiovisual

Justice Play: A Question of Justice is a drama featuring a

jester in the central role questioning common assumptions
about biblical justice. Order from Mennonite Central Committee, 21 South 12th Street, P.O. Box 500, Akron, PA 17501-
0500. Loan only, at no charge.

Chapter 4

Print

Christian:

*Punishment and Retribution: An Attempt to Delimit Their
Scope in New Testament Thought* by C.F.D. Moule, New Perspectives on Crime and Justice: Occasional Paper No. 10. Its
central thesis is ". . . that the word 'punishment' and other
words related to it (especially 'retribution') have, if used in
their strictly correct sense, no legitimate place in the Christian
vocabulary" (p. 3). Order from Mennonite Central Committee,
21 South 12th Street, P.O. Box 500, Akron, PA 17501-0500.
$1.00 single copy; $.40 multiple copies.

** Christ and the Judgment of God: Divine Retribution in the
New Testament* by Stephen H. Travis, Marshall Morgan and
Scott Basingstoke, 1986. Much as with Moule's book, the author argues: "What happens in the New Testament is that [the]
non-retributive understanding of man's relation to God becomes dominant. Retributive concepts are almost displaced
because of the nature of the Christian gospel. It is a gospel
which proclaims Christ as the one through whom people are
invited into relationship with God. Once this relationship to
Christ and to God is seen as central, retributive concepts become inappropriate. The experience described by terms such
as *forgiveness, love* and *acceptance* overrides them. And the
experience of those who refuse to respond to this gospel is not
an experience of retributive punishment, but is the negation
of all that is offered in Christ" (p. 168).

Secular:

Criminology as Peacemaking ed. by Harold E. Pepinsky
and Richard Quinney, Indiana University Press, Bloomington,
1991. The essays in this volume propose peacemaking as an

effective alternative to the "war" on crime. They range from studies of the intellectual roots of the peacemaking tradition to concrete examples of peacemaking in the community. Of special interest are "Reconciliation and the Mutualist Model of Community" (Peter J. Cordella) and "Moving into the New Millennium: Toward a Feminist Vision of Justice" (M. Kay Harris). This book is fairly technical.

Crime, Shame, and Reintegration by John Braithwaite, Cambridge University Press, Cambridge, 1989. Shaming can be counterproductive, making crime problems worse. But when shaming is done within a cultural context of respect for the offender, it can be an extraordinarily powerful, efficient and just form of social control. This book is fairly technical.

Audiovisual
Crime: The Broken Community (see resources for chapter 2).

Chapter 5

Print
Christian:
Monotheism, Power, Justice: Collected Old Testament Essays (see resources for chapter 3). Appropriate to study of chapter 5 is Section II, "Law, Justice and Power," especially the essays, "Law in the Old Testament" and "Theology of Law."

*The Theological Foundation of Law by Jacques Ellul, Seabury Press, New York, 1960. In five divisions, Ellul underscores the ever-present reality of mercy in the application of law.

A Biblical Vison of Justice and More Justice, Less Law (see resources for chapter 3).

Secular:
Law and Revolution: The Formation of the Western Legal Tradition by Harold J. Berman, Harvard University Press, Cambridge, 1983. Part I is of special interest. Highly informative, masterfully researched. Lets us know clearly where our

modern criminal justice system originated, including the decisive influence of the church.

Audiovisual
The resource listed for chapter 3 would also be appropriate for the study of chapter 5.

Chapter 6

Print
Christian:
Changing Lenses: A New Focus for Crime and Justice by Howard Zehr, Herald Press, Scottdale, 1990. Zehr, who is with the Mennonite Central Committee United States Office of Criminal Justice, has written this book, which some are calling a classic on restorative justice. A short version of Zehr's thesis is available as *Retributive Justice, Restorative Justice,* New Perspectives on Crime and Justice: Occasional Paper No. 4 from Mennonite Central Committee. Order from Mennonite Central Committee, 21 South 12th Street, P.O. Box 500, Akron, PA 17501-0500. $1.00 single copy; $.40 multiple copies.

Restorative Justice: Toward Nonviolence by the Rev. Virginia Mackey is a 76-page "Discussion Paper on Crime and Justice" commissioned and distributed by the Presbyterian Criminal Justice Program of the Presbyterian Church (U.S.A.) Excellent! May be ordered from Presbyterian Criminal Justice Program, 100 Witherspoon St., Louisville, KY 40202-1396. No charge.

Secular:
Prison on Trial by Thomas Mathiesen, SAGE Publications, Inc., 1990. The author suggests that the ideology of prison is perpetuated in spite of its overwhelming failure due to three responses from the public sphere. In the widest one, mainly informed through mass media, there reigns a simple non-recognition of the prison fiasco, similar to the millions of Germans who did not 'know' (willfully?) about the Nazi death camps. Within the sphere of criminal justice functionaries, pretense that the prison works in spite of knowledge to the contrary is in place, like the king's attendants in Hans Christian

Andersen's "The Emperor's New Clothes." Among professional criminologists and other researchers, disregard takes over, like the priest and the Levite who passed by the victim on the other side. Mathiesen looks at the international research evidence and concludes that prison is a fiasco even in terms of the rationales of its proponents.

Dialogue on Crime and Punishment: An Educational Project Exploring Community-based Alternatives is an excellent educational kit. Available from The Church Council on Justice and Corrections, CCJC, 507 Bank St., Ottawa, ON K2P 1Z5.

Audiovisual

Crime, Prison and Alternatives (John Howard Society, 1977) is a discussion film in three parts.

Part 1: "Crime the Reality" follows the process of arrest, detention, court appearance, and sentencing.

Part 2: "Prison the Reality" looks at prison and the prison experience for inmates and families.

Part 3: "What Can We Do?" suggests alternatives such as community service orders and Victim Offender Reconciliation Programs.

Available from the Mennonite Central Committee Saskatchewan Office, 600 45th St. W., Saskatoon, SK S7L 5W9. Loan only, at no charge.

Chapter 7

Print

The resources listed for chapter 6 would also be appropriate to the study of chapter 7.

Audiovisual

The Stanford Prison Experiment (slide-tape set) is the record of a classic experiment several years ago which attempted to duplicate the prison experience utilizing college students. The experiment graphically demonstrated the nature of the prison environment and its effects on the keepers as well as the kept. Available from Open Circle, 583 Alice Ave., Rm. 202, Winnipeg, MB R3B 1Z7, or M2/W2 Association, 2825 A

Clearbrook Rd., Clearbrook, BC V2T 2Z3. Loan only, at no charge. Also available from Mennonite Central Committee, 21 South 12th Street, P.O. Box 500, Akron, PA 17501-0500. Loan only, at no charge.

Chapter 8

Print

The resources listed for chapters 2 and 6 would also be appropriate to the study of chapter 8.

Christian:

Dial 911: Peaceful Christians and Urban Violence by Dave Jackson, Herald Press, Scottdale, 1981, discusses ways to respond to crime by drawing upon the experiences of Reba Place Fellowship in Evanston, Illinois. Also, *Dial 911: A Leader's Guide* provides material for using *Dial 911* as a basis for discussion in small groups, Sunday school classes, and the like.

Restorative Justice: Theory; Restorative Justice: Principles, and *Restorative Justice: Practice.* Available from Justice Fellowship, P.O. Box 17181, Washington, DC 20041.

Mediating the Victim Offender Conflict by Howard Zehr is a small booklet which introduces the Victim Offender Reconciliation Program (VORP). Order from Mennonite Central Committee, 21 South 12th Street, P.O. Box 500, Akron, PA 17501-0500. $.40 single copy.

Secular:

Criminal Justice, Restitution and Reconciliation by Burt Galaway and Joe Hudson, Criminal Justice Press, c/o Willow Tree Press, Monsey, New York, 1990. This book and Martin Wright and Burt Galaway's *Mediation and Criminal Justice* (see below) together provide the most important sources of information about Victim Offender Reconciliation Programs currently available.

Mediation and Criminal Justice: Victims, Offenders, and Community ed. by Martin Wright and Burt Galaway, 1989,

SAGE Publications, Inc. P. O. Box 5084, Newbury Park, CA 91359.

Justice: The Restorative Vision by Howard Zehr, Dan Van Ness, and M. Kay Harris, New Perspectives on Crime and Justice: Occasional Paper No. 7 from Mennonite Central Committee. This booklet includes two related, but different visions of restorative justice and a critique. Order from Mennonite Central Committee, 21 South 12th Street, P.O. Box 500, Akron, PA 17501-0500. $1.00 single copy; $.40 multiple copies.

Audiovisual
Crime: The Broken Community and *Crime: Mediating the Conflict* (see resources for chapter 2).

A list of other audiovisual resources, including video versions of television programs on VORP, may be obtained from the U.S. Association for Victim Offender Mediation, c/o PACT, 254 S. Morgan Blvd., Valparaiso, IN 46383; telephone (219) 462-1127.

Chapter 9
Print
Christian:
The resources listed for chapters 2, 6, and 8 would also be appropriate to the study of chapter 9, especially *Changing Lenses: A New Focus for Crime and Justice, Crime and Its Victims: What We Can Do, Justice for Victims and Offenders, Dial 911: Peaceful Christians and Urban Violence.*

Restorative Justice in Ourselves by Katheleen Denison, New Perspectives on Crime and Justice: Occasional Paper No. 11 from Mennonite Central Committee. Examines the work of inner restoration that must accompany "external" restorative justice. Order from Mennonite Central Committee, 21 South 12th Street, P.O. Box 500, Akron, PA 17501-0500. $1.00 single copy; $.40 multiple copies.

Secular:
The resources listed for chapters 2, 6, and 8 would also be appropriate to the study of chapter 9. Also appropriate would

be *Criminology as Peacemaking* (see resources for chapter 4).

Audiovisual

VORP Mediation: A Peacemaking Model is a 20-minute video featuring Ron Claassen's wide experience with VORPs in California. Talking-head, mime, and illustrations combine to offer a clear rationale and procedure for resolving disputes peacefully in a variety of settings. Order from Mennonite Central Committee, 21 South 12th Street, P.O. Box 500, Akron, PA 17501-0500. Purchase for $25; loan at no charge.

* Currently out of print, but may be in your library.

AGREE-DISAGREE SURVEY

1. Anyone who takes seriously the authority of the Bible will support capital punishment on the basis of Genesis 9:6: "Whoever sheds the blood of a human, by a human shall that person's blood be shed; for in his own image God made humankind."

Agree   Disagree

2. "Eye for eye" laws (Exodus 21:22-25; Leviticus 24:18-19; Deuteronomy 19:21) show that God commands revenge as a response to crime.

Agree   Disagree

3. Many Old Testament laws are not to be directly applied today, such as the law authorizing execution of rebellious children (Deuteronomy 21:18-21).

Agree   Disagree

4. To properly apply the Old Testament today, we must listen to the witness of the entire Bible, with the principles of the New Testament taking priority.

Agree   Disagree

5. Not until the New Testament is God revealed to be a God of mercy and love; throughout the Old Testament, God is a God of judgment and vengeance.

Agree   Disagree

You may photocopy this page.

About the Author

Arthur Paul Boers is a Mennonite pastor in Ontario and the author of *On Earth as in Heaven* (Herald Press, 1991). A free-lance writer, he has over 200 articles and reviews published in more than a dozen periodicals, including: *Christianity Today, Gospel Herald, The Mennonite Reporter, Our Family, St. Anthony Messenger, Sojourners,* and *The Windsor Star.* He is a contributing editor for *The Other Side,* a columnist and editorial advisor for *The Christian Ministry,* and writes a column in *Christian Living.*

The oldest child of Dutch immigrants, he was born in Ontario. He received a B.A., majoring in Philosophy, from the University of Western Ontario (1979), an M.A. in Peace Studies from Mennonite Biblical Seminary (1983), and an M.Div. from McCormick Theological Seminary (1988).

In 1980 Arthur married Lorna Jean McDougall, a nurse, and they have two children: Erin Margaret (1984) and Paul Edward (1987). He enjoys reading, walking, bird watching, and the blues.

As well as having volunteered with Victim Offender Reconciliation Program, Arthur serves on the Board of Legal Assistance of Windsor, has consulted with the St. Leonard's Society's Lifeline project, and has co-authored a slide show, *Crime: Mediating the Conflict* (MCC Office of Criminal Justice, 1982).